THE BATTLE OF
POITIERS
1356

THE BATTLE OF
POITIERS
1356

DAVID GREEN

ILLUSTRATIONS BY KATE GREEN

TEMPUS

First published 2002

PUBLISHED IN THE UNITED KINGDOM BY:
Tempus Publishing Ltd
The Mill, Brimscombe Port
Stroud, Gloucestershire GL5 2QG

PUBLISHED IN THE UNITED STATES OF AMERICA BY:
Tempus Publishing Inc.
2 Cumberland Street
Charleston, SC 29401

British Library Cataloguing in Publication Data.
A catalogue record for this book is available from the British Library.

ISBN 0 7524 2557 9

Typesetting and origination by Tempus Publishing.
Printed in Great Britain by Midway Colour Print, Wiltshire

Cover illustration: 'Anglo-Saxon longbowmen' by Kate Green.

CONTENTS

ACKNOWLEDGEMENTS

Much of this was written during a very happy year spent at the University of St Andrews, my thanks to all who made it so.

This has been a collaborative effort. Thanks to Kate for the illustrations and to Alec Green who drew the maps and talked me through some of the logistics of the battle and helped me to clarify several issues. Andrew Midgeley provided many of the photographs and Tweed told me what wargamers want from history (usually more than they should have). Kris Towson helped a great deal with some technical issues and occasional supplies of very decent beer. April and Sally helped me drink it and more besides – for that and all the rest I thank them.

Chris Given-Wilson leant me a copy of his forthcoming book with Françoise Beriac on the prisoners taken at Poitiers for which I'm very thankful.

References have been kept to a minimum and readers are directed to the bibliography if they wish to examine the events of 1355–60 and of the Hundred Years War in more detail. My debt to those authors is clear.

DG

I would like to thank Andy Midgeley for his generous help, support and constant criticism.

KG

Note on the Illustrations

The illustrations are intended to be both representational and acknowledge the style and character of illuminations in (near) contemporary manuscripts of the fourteenth and fifteenth centuries, such as the *Grandes Chroniques*, the *Chroniques* of Jean Froissart and Gaston Fébus' *Livre de chasse*. The colouring and the decorative nature of the manuscripts have been particular influences. Readers are directed towards the very fine online collection held by the Bibliothèque Nationale, Paris, for examples of these rich, atmospheric, and detailed works.

Medieval tapestries such as the Angers Apocalypse and the Lady and the Unicorn (Musée de Cluny) have also influenced the illustrations in terms of texture and means of composition. Further sources have included monumental effigies and brasses. In addition to a range of scholarly literature regarding arms and armour, re-enactments demonstrating the uses of medieval weaponry undertaken by the Royal Armouries have been considered.

Kate Green originally trained as a fine artist at Exeter College of Art and Design and later studied Illustration at Chelsea College of Art and the University of Central England, where she gained a masters degree. She currently works as a decorative artist and book illustrator and has exhibited widely in the UK and Ireland.

List of Illustrations

Illustrations courtesy of David Green unless otherwise stated.

1. Tomb of Sir William Kerdeston. Copyright Andrew Midgeley.
2. Misericord. Copyright Andrew Midgeley.
3. Tomb of Sir Hugh Calveley. Copyright David Green.
4. Henry of Grosmont. Charles Boutell, *The Monumental Brasses of England*, 1847.
5. Mounted man-at-arms. Copyright Kate Green.
6. Statue of Edward the Black Prince. Copyright Andrew Midgeley.
7. Coin of the Black Prince. TA CD 10, 216/285.
8. Coin of the Black Prince. TA CD 10, 217/288.
9. Great Seal of Edward III. Francis Sanford, *A Genealogical History of the Kings of England, Monarchs of Great Britain*, 1671.
10. Seal of Edward, prince of Aquitaine. Francis Sanford, *A Genealogical History of the Kings of England, Monarchs of Great Britain*, 1671.
11. Jupon with the arms of Edward the Black Prince. TA CD 17, 16.
12. Anglo-Welsh longbowmen. Copyright Kate Green.
13. Sir Nicholas Dagworth. Charles Boutell, *The Monumental Brasses of England*, 1847.

COLOUR PLATES

Introduction

The Black Prince and the Hundred Years War

Edward the Black Prince was born at Woodstock in 1330 some seven years before the formal outbreak of the Hundred Years War.[1] The title now given to this conflict is something of a misnomer and one coined by modern historians. It is, of course, flawed mathematically; the traditional dating of the war, from 1337–1453, was a period of 116 years but more significant than this is the broad nature of Anglo-French relations and hostilities in the medieval period. Conflict, although by no means constant, had been endemic long before 1337, in particular as a consequence of the signing of the Treaty of Paris in 1259, and it certainly did not end in 1453 with the fall of Bordeaux. Indeed, the English monarchy maintained its claim to the throne of France until after the revolution of 1789 ensured that there was no crown left for them to seize.

Like the conflict which he shaped and which dictated the course of his brief life and career (he died in 1376), the name by which Edward of Woodstock is best known is the product of a much later age. There is no evidence for it being coined until the sixteenth century; the first example is found in Leland's *Itinerary* and it was used by Raphael Holinshed, whose chronicles were a source for Shakespeare in whose works the prince also appears, as an example and model for Henry V and in his own right in *Edward III*, which has been accepted into the cannon by many scholars in recent years. The idea that the name derived from a penchant for black armour remains unsubstantiated as does the theory that the name was of French origin, brought on by his brutal raids and victories in battle. Nonetheless, the prince's reputation in France was certainly 'black' and is, for example, apparent in the Apocalypse tapestries commissioned by Louis of Anjou in 1373 which are said to depict Edward III as a demon followed by his five sons. Certainly, the *chevauchée* strategy which the English adopted, and which the prince brought to a state of near-perfection in the 1355 raid that burned its way from Bordeaux on the Atlantic coast to Narbonne on the Mediterranean, meant that there was little love for this paragon of chivalry in France.

However, a chivalric archetype he undoubtedly was, for this was not an ethic or code of behaviour that restrained acts of violence against members of the non-knightly classes; on the contrary it may have encouraged them. The chivalric image of the prince is also predicated by the sources that remain of his life, in particular, the chronicles of Jean Froissart, and the first biography of Edward written by the otherwise anonymous Herald of Sir John Chandos. The picture that such evidence paints shows that the foundation of chivalric achievement was military ability, and consequently there is little to choose between the image of the Black Prince as a chivalrous knight and the Black Prince as a victorious general. If the strategy that led to victory involved destroying the reputation and revenue of one's enemy by burning and destroying the land, property and persons of non-combatants then this was, by definition, chivalrous. There is a certain irony in the fact that the Black Prince was to become the near-sovereign ruler of much of the land and the income derived from it that he devastated as well as lord to many of those that he targeted in the raids of 1355 and 1356 and fought against at Poitiers.

The Black Prince is remembered above all as a warrior. Yet, his reputation as a military leader belies the small number of campaigns in which he was involved. He commanded the *chevauchées* of 1355 and 1356 and the Spanish campaign in 1367, but in the Reims expedition (1359–60), as he had been at Crécy (1346), he was, once again, merely a leading player, perhaps a soloist but not the conductor. It appears that he was an extremely capable leader of men and a daring tactician who often enjoyed a Napoleonic element of good fortune on the battlefield. But it is difficult to draw any firm conclusions about his military ability when so few comparisons can be made. The Black Prince and the men under his command, particularly his chief captains and lieutenants (several of whom are described in further detail in Appendix 2), were part of a broad English strategy orchestrated by Edward III. This strategy included both the broad outlines of foreign policy but also the specific military developments which allowed the English (and Anglo-Welsh/Anglo-Gascon) armies to build a reputation that saw them rise from the low ebb that was the defeat at Bannockburn in 1314 to the triumphs of Crécy and Poitiers and to the status of the finest warriors in Europe. The army led by the Black Prince in 1356 reflected these wider trends in many ways, in its recruitment, provisioning, strategy and tactics. However, since he was the heir-apparent and many of the members of his retinue were figures of national military importance, the retinue did not simply follow trends but also set them.

As a consequence, the example of the Black Prince was in many ways representative of the English experience in the Hundred Years War. He fought in the vanguard at the battle of Crécy aged sixteen. He participated in the extended siege of Calais (1346–47), which followed the battle. Calais may seem to be a minor acquisition after such a comprehensive victory and in some ways it was, but the coastal town provided an excellent base for future military incursions and also became a major trade centre when the wool staple was transferred there. The town provided the forum for another smaller scale encounter in 1350. The celebrated French knight Geoffrey de Charny offered Aimery of Pavia, governor of Calais, 20,000 crowns to betray the town in late October 1349. Aimery passed on the news to Edward III and under the banner of Walter Manny, Edward III and the Black Prince with Guy Brian and others successfully ambushed the attackers.

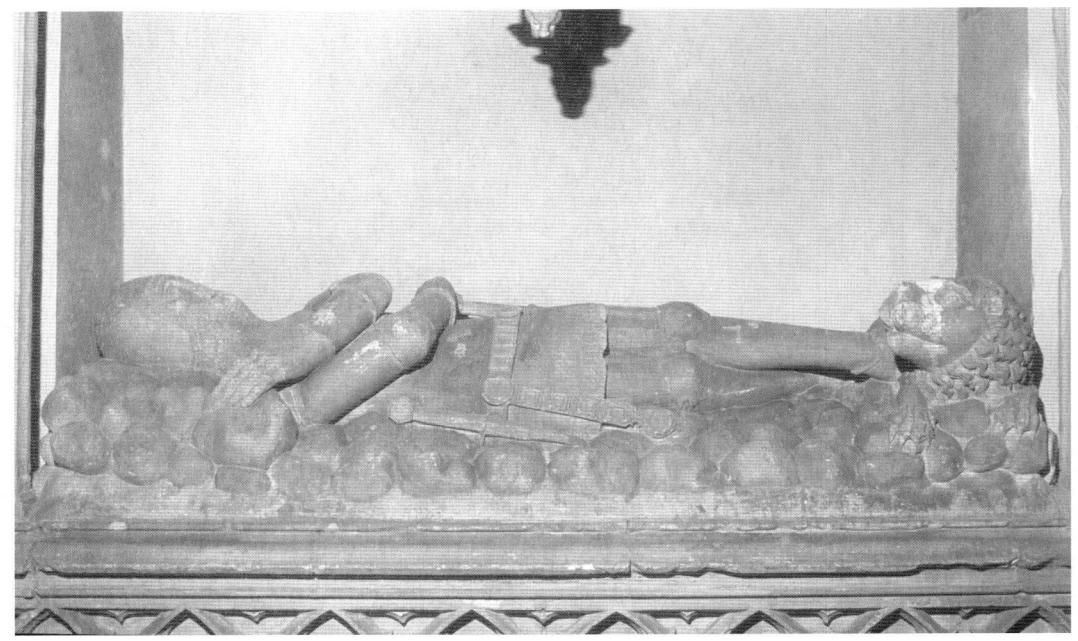

1. Tomb of Sir William Kerdeston, Reepham, Norfolk. Kerdeston was one of the Black Prince's Norfolk retainers. He fought as a banneret in the vanguard at Crécy and brought reinforcements to the siege of Calais in 1347. He was also MP for Norfolk between 1337 and 1344 and again in 1360. He died on 14 August 1361. His tomb shows the knight lying in a slightly contorted manner on rocks and boulders. This may reflect some changes in funerary monuments after the Black Death, revealing the painful nature of life, but it is possible that this is a more romantic image showing the chivalric adventurer lost in a mythical forest.

Further military action was curtailed by the devastation and social dislocation wrought by the Black Death and intense diplomatic activity marked the years until 1355 when the prince and others led a number of devastating raids deep into the French countryside. In the following year the indignities being heaped upon the French were compounded when the prince captured Jean II, 'the Good', king of France, at the battle of Poitiers.

This marked the point at which the prince truly took his place on the European stage and it led to the treaty of Brétigny-Calais of 1360. This was concluded after the failure of the English attempts to capture first Reims and then Paris with the aim of having Edward III crowned king of France in place of the absent and captive Jean. The resolution was an agreement

2. Misericord – showing heraldic devices of the Black Prince and the duke of Brittany, King's Lynn, Norfolk. The Hundred Years War brought many conflicts and struggles within its orbit, the contest for the duchy of Brittany being one of these. The Black Prince and several of his retinue including John Chandos were closely involved in support of Jean de Montfort against the Valois-sponsored candidate, Charles de Blois. The arms of the prince and Montfort are here seen together on a misericord in the church of St Margaret, King's Lynn. After the prince's death, Montfort was granted his property in Lynn and the nearby estate of Castle Rising.

involving a king's ransom and the transfer of sovereignty over nearly a third of the kingdom of France to Edward III. Much of this was entrusted to his eldest son who, in addition to his many lands and titles in England and Wales, acquired the principality of Aquitaine.

The agreement of 1360 was a serious attempt to conclude the war but it was flawed and in time contributed as much to the continuity of the struggle as it did to its brief resolution. Indeed, when Henry V embarked on the campaign that would conclude at Agincourt, he did so with the expressed intent to acquire that which he felt was still owed from the treaty of Brétigny. While the failures of diplomacy continued to fan the flames of the Hundred Years War it was also fuelled by many other lesser and regional conflicts that came within its orbit. These also provided a broader stage on which the war could be fought. In a sense, the Hundred Years War was a war between the French principalities and great feudatories, led by the king of England in his capacity as duke of Gascony. Charles 'the Bad' of Navarre was also a continual thorn in the flesh of the French monarchy as he sought to play off Valois against Plantagenet to his own advantage. At the battle of Cocherel on 16 May 1364, the up-and-coming French commander Bertrand du Guesclin defeated a Navarrese army assisted by some English and Gascon troops led by Jean de Grailly, the captal de Buch, a key Gascon supporter of England who was captured.

The duchy of Brittany provided another area of friction. A war of succession between Charles de Blois and Jean de Montfort allowed the protagonists to secure the support of France and England on their respective sides. In this conflict the prince played a political and diplomatic role and a number of his retinue and household took a more direct part. John Chandos led Montfort's troops at the clash at Auray on 29 September 1364. He was aided by Robert Knolles, Hugh Calveley and others who successfully combated experimental French tactics and troop dispositions designed to counteract the efficiency of Montfort's archers. At Auray the tight formations of the Anglo-Breton forces triumphed in the mêlée which witnessed the death of Charles de Blois and (not the first) capture of du Guesclin.

These 'extraneous' hostilities as well as the central conflict were characterised by the heavy use of mercenary forces. The Anglo-French war was, of course, not the first time that merce-naries were used on the battlefield but the endemic nature of the conflict and the variety of theatres in which it could take place provided a great number of employers and opportunities. By contrast, the 'cold war' period from 1360 (particularly after the death of Blois at Auray) until the reopening of the war in 1369 created a pool of unwanted military labour and the unemployed Free Companies continued to raid and ravage the French coun-tryside in this period. This was no minor inconvenience and hit hard a country that had already suffered the depredations of twenty years of English raiding, the social, demographic and financial effects of the Black Death, the Jacquerie and the fiscal implications of funding urban defences and paying the ransom

3. Tomb of Sir Hugh Calveley, Bunbury church, Cheshire. Calveley was one of a number of Cheshire *routiers* who found employment in the Hundred Years War. He fought at Poitiers with the Black Prince and later was closely involved in Iberian affairs. He played a leading role in both the deposition and subsequent reinstatement of Pedro the Cruel to the throne of Castile.

resulting from the capture of Jean at Poitiers, some 3 million crowns. A Castilian civil war provided a solution to this problem and the opportunity for King Charles V (after his father's death in 1364) to establish an ally on the southern border of the principality of Aquitaine, an ally who also controlled the most powerful galley fleet operating in northern European waters.

It was from his principality of Aquitaine that the prince launched the English response. It was to be his last campaign and he secured his final victory at the battle of Nájera by which he restored the English–allied Pedro I to the throne of Castile, a throne from which he had recently been deposed by Bertrand du Guesclin, soon to be constable of France, and the mercenary Free Companies. The battle of Nájera in 1367 was a close-run affair partly as a consequence of the tactical ability of du Guesclin who demanded better armour for the Trastamaran forces and attempted to counter the English combination of archers and infantry by making his knights fight on foot.

Victory for the prince and Pedro, however, was short-lived, for the latter in a very literal sense – he was murdered by his half-brother, Enrique, at Montiel in 1369. A different fate awaited Edward when he returned, broken with the illness which would eventually claim his life, and bankrupt, to Gascony which, as it had formed the main reason for the outbreak of the Hundred Years War, so it provided the opportunity and the forum for it restarting in 1369. This followed an appeal by the nobility of the greater Aquitaine to the king of France and the *parlement* of Paris regarding the prince's style of government and imposition of taxes, although the underlying causes were certainly more complex than these. The result of the revolt was the loss of nearly all that the English had gained in the years since the war began in 1337.

Edward returned home following the siege of Limoges, the last military action in which he participated although his health was such that he directed the assault on the city from a litter. The prince's personal tragedy was underlined by the death of his eldest son, Edward of Angoulême. His last years were ones of uneven decline. He may have taken a greater interest in matters of domestic politics but it is more likely that his name and reputation were playing their part rather than the prince taking an active role. He died in the midst of the Good Parliament in 1376.

1

THE *GRANDE CHEVAUCHÉE* OF 1355

In 1346, before the Crécy campaign, it had been an appeal for military assistance that led to an English expedition in France. So it was once more in 1355. In January, certain members of the Gascon nobility including Jean de Grailly, the captal de Buch (so-called because of the hereditary title he bore, to the *captalate* of Buch) and the lords of Lesparre and Mussidan were present in England at the birth of Edward III's son, Thomas. There they expressed their deep concern at the hostile activities of the count of Armagnac. As one of the most important members of the nobility of southern France, Jean d'Armagnac had been appointed the French king's lieutenant in Languedoc in November 1352. He had not proved to be an amicable neighbour and two months later he began military action against English Gascony with the siege of Saint-Antonin. This pressure continued for some time and he made considerable inroads into the duchy so that by the end of May 1354, Armagnac was encamped only 27 leagues from Bordeaux on the banks of the River Lot.

This particular attack on the duchy of Gascony was also set against a general backdrop of conflict. Formal activity in the Hundred Years War had been limited after the fall of Calais to the English in 1347, partly because of the disruption caused by the Black Death (1347/8–50), and there had been ongoing attempts at diplomacy to seek a resolution although these had been unsuccessful. The most significant of these had been the failure of the French to ratify the treaty of Guînes and the breakdown of subsequent negotiations at Avignon. Accordingly, the Gascon wish for a response to Armagnac's attacks merely set the seal on the resumption of Anglo-French hostilities.

RECRUITMENT

The Black Prince's expedition in 1355 marked his first independent command and the size and quality of his personal retinue and household was indicative of his importance and authority as a military commander, and more significantly as the heir-apparent of England and, if his father's foreign policy came to fruition, France. The expeditionary force was made up of members of his household, his retainers, annuitants and the retinues of those magnates who followed him.

The English military 'machine' had undergone something of a transformation, perhaps even a revolution since it had been taught a bitter lesson in many battles with the Scots, the most painful of which had been delivered at Bannockburn. By 1355, English armies were not recruited by recourse to the traditional 'feudal' demand for military service. Rather, recruiting captains would be employed by means of indentures – contracts which specified the number and types of troops they were to supply for a particular campaign or particular period of campaigning. The conditions of service were laid out including issues concerning payment, booty and dates and points of embarkation. Such agreements, which might be taken out for an individual or a whole army were indicative of the increasingly professional attitude of the English.

If the means of bringing an army into the field was innovative, the broad strategy that the army would implement was not. Raiding had been one of the most common forms of warfare throughout the medieval period but the degree of sophistication, organisation and devastation that the Anglo-Gascon army brought to this military tradition was something new. The English intended to cause extreme levels of economic and social disloca-tion and damage through the raiding tactics of the *chevauchée*. If this drew out the enemy then they had developed an effective strategic and tactical plan should they need to fight a battle. In order to implement this, the right kind of troops, properly equipped and supplied, were necessary. It is no surprise that the driving force behind the development of English taxation systems and governmental and bureaucratic processes which occurred in the later middle ages was warfare and the need to provide the resources for this evolved form of military operation.

On 10 July 1355, the prince signed an indenture with his father which outlined the responsibilities of those involved with the campaign. This specified that the prince was to lead a force of 433 men-at-arms (although this may have been exceeded), 400 mounted archers and 300 foot archers totalling 1,133 soldiers. This was to be supplemented by troops under the command of the earls of Warwick, Suffolk, Oxford and Salisbury, Sir John Lisle and Sir Reginald Cobham. Taking into account the advance payments made to the captains around the same time, it is probable that the prince led a total force of 2,600 although the final figure may have been slightly higher. There are no extant muster rolls for the 1355 expedition, but some reconstruction of the army can be made through shipping records which indicate that Warwick, Suffolk, Oxford, Salisbury, Lisle and Cobham probably brought 500 men-at-arms and 800 archers. In addition to those recruited by the prince, this gives a total of 933 men-at-arms and 1,800 archers to which were added about 1,000 Gascons from the duchy. This force would be further supple-mented by the retinues of the Gascon nobility who joined the prince on the expedition.[1]

The first indications that there would be a campaign, at least in terms of recruiting troops for the purpose, pre-dated the formal signing of the indenture and began in the prince's earldom of Chester. In May and June 1355, 500 archers were to be 'chosen, tested and arrayed' along with 100 from Flintshire. They were contracted to arrive at Plymouth, the point of embarkation, 'by three weeks before Midsummer' and it appears that all but forty of these did so. Cheshire archers, probably due to national leanings rather than an indication of military skill, received a higher rate of pay than the Welsh soldiers who were employed as both archers and light infantry, armed with lances and pikes.[2]

In contrast to the Crécy-Calais campaign, there was only a small Welsh contingent in the prince's army in 1355. These were attached to the prince's own household retinue. Gronou ap Griffith commanded sixty men from north Wales, and David ap Blethin Vaghan, thirty men from Flintshire. Three notable Welsh knights also brought their retinues; John Griffith, Rhys ap Griffith, who may have been the leader of a force from south Wales with the third, Hywel ap Griffith, known to posterity as Sir Hywel of the Axe. This was the first campaign in the Hundred Years War in which the Welsh were recorded as using horses.[3]

Wages of war and 'regard' (an advance payment)
were received by the following:

Prince of Wales	£8,129 18s.
Earl of Warwick	£2,614 4s.
Earl of Suffolk	£1,428 6s. 8d.
Earl of Oxford	£1,174 13s. 10d.
Earl of Salisbury	£1,124 2s. 2d.
Reginald Cobham	£652 0s. 8d.

As well as a considerable administrative and logistical exercise, this was a major financial undertaking. The advance cost of the expedition including war wages and payment of 'regard' was some £19,500, and shipping a further £3,300. In the year from September 1355, over £55,000 was spent on the prince's military operation in Gascony.[4]

The prince was sent to Gascony to lead a military expedition but he also had a governmental, political and diplomatic role. He was to serve as his father's lieutenant in the duchy and was provided with financial resources 'for the conciliation of the people of the country' and authority to make ordinances and act 'as he shall think best for the honour and profit of the king in all matters... in the duchy of Gascony'. Furthermore, in the event of the prince being besieged or beset by overwhelming forces, he was to be sent reinforcements by the king in person and/or the duke of Lancaster, and earls of Arundel, Northampton, March and Stafford. This was to be a national expedition, resourced by the Crown and supported by the most powerful magnates of the realm, but the inherent dangers were also recognised and the potential threat of the loss or capture of the heir-apparent was given due consideration.

The force that left England in 1355 was small compared with that which marched to Crécy although it was complemented on arrival by Gascon forces and further increased prior to the 1356 expedition when Sir Richard Stafford, one of the prince's key retainers, was commissioned to reinforce and re-supply the army.

Evidence for the Gascon participants in 1355 and 1356 is also not as comprehensive as one would wish. Despite the continuity of records in Gascony in the period 1354–61, those for the 1355 campaign and Gascon contingents are not complete.[5] It is clear nonetheless, that several members of the local nobility led military companies and some had seen action in English service in the past. Despite the chequered nature of Gascon relations with the English crown over many years, the political and military integrity of the duchy was to a greater or lesser degree dependent on the support of the local aristocracy. In this context, without any other motivation, it is clear to see why the appeal of the Gascon nobility to Edward III in the face of the threat from Armagnac and Clermont, was successful. The captal de Buch, an established supporter of the English cause, was among those who appealed for assistance in January 1355. To further strengthen his loyalty, Edward III granted him various rights and perquisites, mainly in the towns of Bénauges and Ilaz. In addition, members of the Albret family: Amauri de Biron, sire de Montferrand; Auger de Montaut, sire de Mussidan; Guillaume de Pommiers; Guillaume Sans, sire de Lesparre; and Guillaume Amanier, sire de Roson all led troops in the campaigns of 1355–56.

THE COMMANDERS

The chief commanders and officers of the 1355 expedition were closely associated with the prince's household and personal

4. Henry of Grosmont, duke of Lancaster, KG, 1299–1361 (from the Hastings brass). One of the finest military commanders of the late middle ages, he led numerous campaigns in the war and was involved in vital diversionary expeditions in 1346 and 1356.

retinue. Among the magnates, Robert Ufford, earl of Suffolk, was the titular head of the prince's council and had been associated with him since 1338 and William Montague, earl of Salisbury, had been knighted with the prince when they had landed at La Hogues in 1346. In addition to Warwick, Lisle and Cobham the leaders included James Audley, Richard Stafford, John Chandos, John Wingfield, Baldwin Botetourt, Bartholomew Burghersh, Nigel Loryng, Stephen Cosington, Roger Cotesford, Alan Cheyne and William Trussel. These were men of considerable military experience in the wars with France and Scotland and there were several that had fought in Gascony and understood something of its characteristics and peculiarities. Among these, Loryng, Audley and Stafford had served with Henry of Grosmont, then earl of Derby, in 1345.

The military talent at the prince's disposal was evident in the fact that the army contained seven knights of the Garter and, in Ufford and Cobham the constable were two who would later be included among its ranks. So it was that among the leaders of the army at least a dozen had fought at Crécy and others in Gascony in 1345–46. The bonds formed from a year campaigning together would compound these associations and experience to make the prince's retinue an extremely effective military force.[6]

In addition to the purely military arm of the prince's entourage, much of his domestic household also rode with him and their peacetime function was amended to incorporate campaigning duties both for the prince himself and the army at large. The prince's household staff included Nicholas Bonde (squire), Henry Aldrington (master-tailor), William Bakton (yeoman of the buttery), Richard Doxeye (baker), Robert Egremont (pavillioner), Geoffrey Hamelyn (keeper of the prince's armour), John Henxteworth (controller of the household), William Lenche (porter), and Henry Berkhamsted (porter, later constable of Berkhamsted castle). Through the activities of these men, the campaign was organised and administered by the prince's staff. He appears to have valued their service highly since officers of the household received money gifts to a total of £275 10s. as a result of their efforts in outfitting the expedition to Gascony.[7]

The roles that all these men played in the daily organisation of the army and in terms of the command structure can be partially reconstructed from evidence contained within a number of campaign letters. These were part of an ongoing propaganda campaign that appears to have been relatively successful in ensuring public support and, more importantly, public money for the war with France. These communications sent back by Edward and others indicate that Audley, Chandos, Botetourt and, at times, Burghersh:

> were the prince's handy men for field work, that Stafford was assigned to special tasks (as he had been before the campaign), that Wingfield remained as 'head of the office' and that these men who had of course known one another before going out to France, formed a group bound by friendly relations to one another and by common loyalty to their chief: they were part of the 'permanent staff'.[8]

PREPARATION AND TRANSPORT

The indenture of 10 June 1355, in addition to outlining the troops to be recruited for the expedition, also detailed the means by which the army was to travel to Gascony and undertake the *chevauchée* once it arrived there. It included specifications for the purchase of horses, the provision of ships and such lesser matters as the purveyance of hurdles (used for separating horses when onboard ship). Thomas Hoggeshawe, lieutenant of John Beauchamp, the admiral of the fleet west of the Thames, was appointed acting commander of the prince's fleet and John Deyncourt, sub-admiral of the northern fleet, was also involved. General orders regarding the impending expedition were sent out as early as April: Henry Keverell, presumably a merchant or supplier of ships and boats, was paid for the purchase of gear for the prince's ship; items were delivered to John le Clerk and his fellows, the keepers of the *Christophre*, the ship aboard which the prince was to travel; and on 16 July, ships from Bayonne were impounded (or 'arrested' as it was described) in various ports.[9] Some of these vessels had previously been used to transport Henry of Lancaster's troops to Normandy where he was to be engaged in a campaign in the hope that a twin-pronged assault would divide

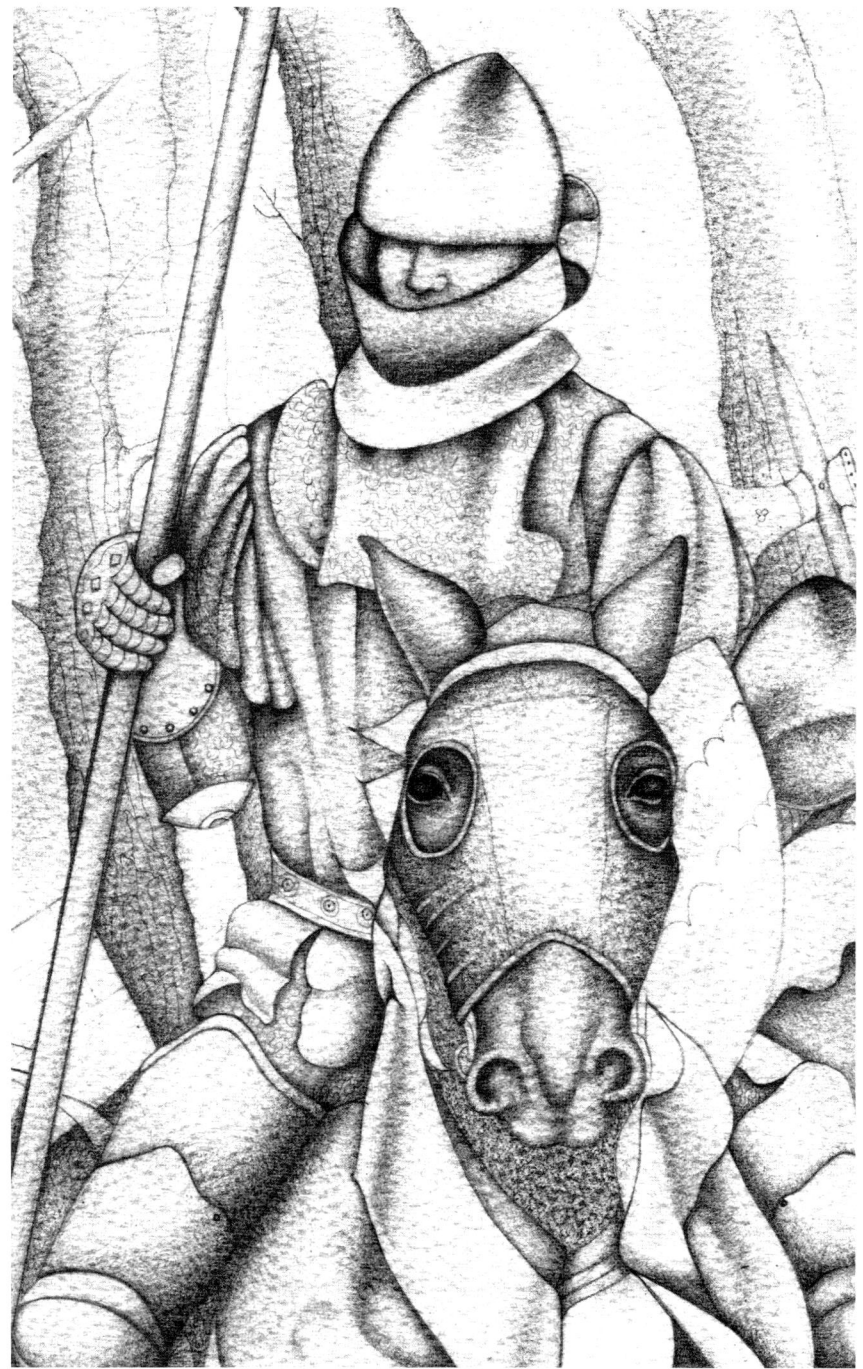

5. Mounted man-at-arms.

French royal forces between the north and the south.[10] Letters of safe conduct were issued to the prince's men from 8 June and as late as 6 September. It seems that preparations were undertaken with the intention that the expeditionary force should arrive in Gascony very soon after the expiration of the Anglo-French truce on 24 June. However, in the event, contrary winds and perhaps delays in securing sufficient numbers of ships prevented departure until the second week of September. During the delay at Plymouth the prince stayed at Plympton priory and concerned himself with affairs regarding the duchy of Cornwall. An advance party led by Tiderick van Dale, usher of the prince's chamber, and Bartholomew Burghersh the younger, was sent over soon after 1 July prior to the arrival the main fleet and Stephen Cosington and William the Chaplain prepared the archbishop's palace at Bordeaux for the prince who stayed there, whilst not on campaign, until his return to England in 1357. The main fleet sailed on 8/9 September and arrived in Bordeaux eight days later at the height of the *vendange*. The earls of Warwick and Suffolk and their retinues embarked and sailed from Southampton.[11]

On 21 September, the prince was presented to the great and the good of the duchy. He spoke before the nobles of Gascony and the citizens of Bordeaux: his appointment as the king's lieutenant was proclaimed and his father's letters and commands were read out in a ceremony conducted in considerable splendour in the cathedral of St Andrew.[12]

LES CAVALIERS DE L'APOCALYPSE[13]

Following as it did on the heels of the Black Death, the *chevauchée* of 1355 was a catastrophe for the people of southern France who were caught up in it. The Black Prince's reputation (and perhaps, consequently, his pseudonym) was founded on the raid from Bordeaux to Narbonne and it was such a raid that was depicted in the Angers Apocalypse tapestries of Louis of Anjou. The prince was to be only one of the horsemen, however. As had been the strategy in 1346, the campaign was preceded by an attempt to divide French forces. Henry of Grosmont was again involved and on this occasion he attacked Normandy with

6. Statue of Edward the Black Prince, Leeds City Square. The statue was commissioned in recognition of Leeds gaining city status at the turn of the twentieth century. The prince was seen, somewhat strangely, as a symbol of good government. The equestrian image is much more in keeping with the military reputation he gained at the battles of Crécy and Poitiers.

Charles of Navarre, while the prince was to ride from Gascony. It is possible that there was a third element to the plan and that King Edward himself may have led a limited *chevauchée* into the French interior.

No attempts at secrecy preceded the attack led by the prince in 1355. Hostilities had already broken out between Armagnac and the Gascons and the raid from Bordeaux was to be merely one element in a wider operation; French forces would be divided if they tried to deal with the king, the prince and Lancaster simultaneously.

The army left Bordeaux by 5 October, its strength augmented by the contingents led by the Gascon nobility, probably numbering a further 4,000 men, which brought the total force to between 6,000 and 8,000 troops. It marched south and a little east before heading almost due east on reaching Plaissance. Thereafter the raid continued to the Mediterranean coast and Narbonne. The return to Bordeaux followed a not dissimilar path, widening the band of destruction to encompass Limoux, Boulbonne and Gimont. The raid proved to be a remarkable exercise in devastation and destruction. It was perhaps the pre-eminent example of the *chevauchée* strategy. It was an expedition that led from the Atlantic to the Mediterranean and back, which was aimed at the economic resources and the credibility of the Valois monarchy in the south and that assaulted over 500 villages, towns, castles and other settlements and strongholds.

When nearing Arouille, following usual practice the army divided into three columns in order to march on a broad front to maximise the damage that might be caused. Anglo-Gascon casualties were low throughout the 1355 raid but there was a notable exception at this point in the operation when John Lord Lisle fell at Estang. Lisle had a long history of distinguished service. In 1339 and the early 1340s he had served in Gascony with Derby and he had fought at Crécy. In recognition of this he became a founder member of the Order of the Garter. He had also been involved in the naval encounter at Winchelsea and such service may well have contributed to his appointment as sheriff of Cambridgeshire and Huntingdonshire and governor of Cambridge castle.[14] Military service often led to public duties in the shires and, increasingly, in the service of central government as well as in parliament, amongst whose members were many old soldiers.

The increasing bureaucratisation of the English government meant that it was becoming ever more possible to forge a career and to seek personal advantage and patronage by rendering service in activities outside the military sphere. Nonetheless, military service was still one of the chief means of social and professional advancement and the giving of titles and promotions was a regular feature of the 1355 campaign. Richard Stafford was made a banneret at Bassoues on 19 October and a number of new knights were dubbed including William Stratton, the prince's tailor, and Tiderick van Dale on 12 November.

After marching south for a hundred miles, the army swung east, crossed the River Gers, which marked Armagnac's eastern border, and approached the count's headquarters at Toulouse. At this stage in the expedition, the larger towns tended to be avoided while those less well defended were pillaged and burned. This was not a siege train but a swiftly moving raid of devastation. The army forded the Garonne to the south and then the Ariège. This was a highly audacious move, 'an unthinkable idea to those who knew the area, and one which does not seem to have occurred to Armagnac... [who] was confident that the Anglo-Gascons would not be able to penetrate into Languedoc beyond Toulouse.' The count was not drawn out and the army arrived at Carcassonne on 2 November. The city attempted to bribe the prince with 250,000 gold *écus*. It was not accepted and the *bourg* (the outer town) was burned, although no attempt was made on the heavily defended *cité* (the fortified, administrative centre). Narbonne, which they reached on 8 November, provided even less resistance and although the citadel similarly held out, the town was virtually uninhabited and undefended when the prince arrived. Edward stayed in the Carmelite convent while the rest of the town was looted, albeit while suffering attack and bombardment from the *cité*; they withdrew on 10 November, pursued by furious troops and townsmen.

Two French armies began to converge on the prince at this point from Toulouse and Limoges led by Armagnac and Jacques de Bourbon respectively. The Marshal Clermont also brought troops from north of the Dordogne and further support was expected from the Dauphin until he was diverted to Picardy. The prince marched north crossing the Aude at Aubian and, when approached, the French fell back. Armagnac's policy was that of Philip VI before the battle of Crécy, and with better reason because of it. He aimed therefore to defend the principal river crossings, towns and fortified sites. Prior to leaving Narbonne, the prince received letters from the pope who was fearful of the intentions of an army not far from Avignon. The messengers were not received courteously and after a considerable wait were told to address their concerns to the king.

The march back was determined by the proximity of Armagnac and Bourbon and the prince's motivation is uncertain. Was he seeking a battle or trying to avoid one? Edward rode in the direction of Béziers before turning east, perhaps in the face of French reinforcements, towards Armagnac. The prince was certainly expecting a battle even if he was not trying to engineer an encounter, but Armagnac continued to withdraw. The prince followed him as far as Carcassonne and then headed towards the comparative safety of the lands of the count of Foix. 15 November marked an iconic moment in the raid and indeed the whole *chevauchée* strategy: Edward and his commanders spent the day at the Dominican house at Prouille, it being Sunday, while the rest of the army burned four towns in twelve hours.

The prince met Gaston Fébus, count of Foix, on 17 November at Boulbonne and an agreement was reached between them so that Gaston's lands were to be spared any attack or disruption. While officially neutral, Gaston assisted the prince, 'non seulement il assura son ravitaillement, mais encore il permit aux Béarnais de s'engager dans le corps expeditionnaire.'[15] The route back to Gascony was difficult and treacherous, taken perhaps in an attempt to avoid Armagnac although if the count tried to engage Edward it was not until he crossed the Ariège. There was some fierce but limited skirmishing and the army re-entered the duchy on 28 November and reached La Réole on 2 December.

Armagnac's failure to react to the prince's army is very peculiar considering the extent of the destruction and the possible prizes should he win a battle. Hewitt argued, 'It is most probable that he had a secret understanding with the English', but there seems to be little evidence to support this view and far more to suggest that he was a loyal Valois subject. In any case, the avoidance of pitched battle was extremely common due to the very great risk of capture and casualties should the encounter be lost. The association of the prince with the count of Foix must have given him pause for thought. Furthermore, there are no accurate figures concerning the forces that he had at his disposal and he may have been greatly outnumbered.[16]

The raids of 1355–56, like that which preceded the encounter at Crécy, struck at the military and personal reputation of the French monarch and nobility and seriously affected royal tax revenue. Like those that had happened before, the *grande chevauchée* was deliberately destructive, extremely brutal and all the more so since it was methodical and sophisticated. After the conclusion of the expedition, Sir John Wingfield, the prince's business manager, wrote to the bishop of Winchester. His letter, often quoted, shows great concern with determining the exact value to the French crown of the areas that were overrun in 1355 and thus the extent of the economic damage that was being caused.[17]

> For the countryside and towns which have been destroyed in this raid produced more revenue for the king of France in aid of his wars than half his kingdom;... as I could prove from authentic documents found in various towns in the tax collectors' houses.[18]

The 1355 expedition was an archetypal *chevauchée* and proved to be a remarkable tactical and logistical achievement. The prince marched from the Atlantic to the Mediterranean coast and back fighting only a few minor skirmishes and causing a vast amount of damage. French defensive preparations were generally ineffective and over 500 settlements were burned, it was 'une catastrophe sans précédent.'[19]

2

WINTER/SPRING 1355–56 – DEFENCE AND PREPARATION

During the winter of 1355–56, the troops were billeted along the northern march. Warwick remained at La Réole, Salisbury went to Saint-Foy, and Suffolk to Saint-Emilion. The prince, with Chandos and Audley, marched to Libourne. Three weeks passed before any further action was undertaken.[1]

The need for public support and particularly that of parliament for the war effort encouraged the development of a sophisticated programme of propaganda. This took several forms from stained glass images, manuscript illuminations, a variety of public ceremonies and pageants and proclamations to such august organisations as the Order of the Garter. It became the practice to send regular communication back from the front to England for purposes of propaganda and informing a range of different public audiences. In some cases these also included personal letters. The 1355–56 expedition was no different and such documents are extremely valuable, providing a great deal of information about the period between the *grande chevauchée* and the raid that would lead to a battlefield outside Poitiers.[2]

7. Coin of the Black Prince.

Two letters were later written at Bordeaux on 23 and 25 December 1355 by the prince and John Wingfield (governor of the prince's business affairs) to William Edington, bishop of Winchester. Edington was the head of the prince's council in England and communications that were sent initially to the prince's officials were then circulated more widely throughout the country. Wingfield also wrote at Libourne on 22 January, probably to Richard Stafford, who had travelled back to England bearing letters and with a commission to return with reinforcements and supplies. This communication related events subsequent to the first raid.[3] Later, other letters were dispatched, three of which remain, which recounted the events of the second raid and the battle of Poitiers. That of 25 June 1356, sent to the bishop of Hereford, was brief and requested prayers and masses. On 20 October, Roger Cotesford, one of the prince's bachelors, took a letter to the bishop of Worcester. The most important missive was carried by Nigel Loryng to the mayor, aldermen and commonality of London and was probably also intended for subsequent distribution outside the capital.[4] Other members of the retinue who wrote home also passed information. Bartholomew Burghersh penned communications to John Beauchamp, and Henry Peverel corresponded with the prior of Winchester. The prince also wrote to the prior naming all those killed or captured at Poitiers. News was also passed by papal envoys, via the wine trade, and by the sub-admirals Deyncourt and Hoggeshawe who returned with some of the ships which had taken the army to Gascony.[5] Requests for prayers continued to be made regularly. The Friars Preachers, Friars Minor, Carmelites and Austin friars, and the bishop of London were contacted with this demand.

In its propaganda programme the crown relied heavily on the services of the church and the parochial system became the chief conduit for the distribution of news through sermons and prayers that were said for the success of English armies in France. The Hundred Years War was a 'just war' for both English and French according to the principles of Augustine and later commentators. This not only 'justified' the shedding of blood but also further emphasised that triumph in battle was an indication of divine approbation for the victors. Prior to his departure in 1355 the prince had visited Westminster to pray for success in the forthcoming expedition. On his return from Poitiers, the prince gave thanks for his victory at Canterbury.

During the winter and spring of 1355–56 the prince was concerned with a number of matters as well as the forthcoming campaign. In his capacity as the king's lieutenant there were also administrative concerns to deal with such as an appeal of the commonality of Bayonne against the count of Albret and diplomatic contacts had to be maintained with the count of Foix.[6]

While the prince busied himself with the affairs of the duchy, Sir Richard Stafford returned to England and Wales with a commission to bring reinforcements and supplies. The exact details of his mission are uncertain. Much of the recruiting was done in Cheshire where it appears that he brought over 300 archers into service. This was probably fewer than had been hoped. The duke of Lancaster was also recruiting troops at this time which placed further pressure on the availability of manpower. Perhaps nearly 300 further longbowmen were recruited from other areas. Military summons were also sent to the seneschals of north Wales. In addition to those troops from the prince's demesne, the expedition attracted men from Westmoreland and Yorkshire, as well as Germany.[7]

In Gascony, the immediate concern was with defence and fortification. The frontiers of the duchy were extended and fortified, a task simplified by the support, won and induced financially, of a number of Gascon nobles who had not participated in the earlier campaign, including Jean de Galard, Bertrand de Durfort and the lords of Caumont and Chalais. The army was deployed along the frontier and, under the command of some of the key figures in the military retinue, a number of small-scale raids were made. The distribution of forces along the borders was a useful defensive measure against counter-attacks as well as serving to enlarge the Anglo-Gascon 'Pale' and it may have reduced any tensions that existed within the army. Despite this, however, the French retook over thirty towns and castles.[8] The difficulties of defending the borders of Gascony would be multiplied many times over when the Black Prince attempted to maintain the political integrity of the much larger principality of Aquitaine. However, for the moment there were also other, more opaque considerations. When the army had ridden through Languedoc it had been at liberty to burn and destroy. Now it occupied 'not only the physical borderland between English and French territory, but also the moral and legal borderland between the warrior and the armed criminal.' A much more careful distinction had to be made between non-combatants of English and French territory who, respectively, had the right to protection or who might be killed and robbed.[9]

During the spring of 1356 the policy was to harass the enemy, possibly whilst waiting for reinforcements, or a further English invasion elsewhere, or perhaps simply until the weather improved. The raids had begun around Christmas. In Saintonge the front probably lay along the River Charente, from Rochefort (threatening La Rochelle) to Taillebourg and as far as Cognac where Burghersh was stationed. From there he raided northward into Poitou and perhaps beyond. The captal de Buch was particularly successful, recapturing a number of castles in the east of Saintonge before invading Poitou in January and turning south toward Périgeux which he took and handed over to the lord of Mussidan. In the region of the Dordogne, the operational headquarters were at Libourne with reserves at St Emilion. The earls of Oxford, Salisbury and Suffolk with Elie de Pommiers and the lord of Mussidan, commanded 1,000 men and raided across the valley of the river towards Rocamadour. They took Souillac and

8. Coin of the Black Prince.

Beaulieu-sur-Dordogne. The Garonne formed another boundary, although the French had some garrisons west of the river. Warwick probably crossed somewhere near Port Sainte Marie, which was captured by a detachment under the command of Chandos and Audley in January 1356. Warwick then swung northwards along the right-hand bank of the Garonne. Clairac was also taken before he marched on and captured Tonneins. At the time of Wingfield's letter he was near Marmande. Chandos and Audley turned to the Agenais. They took Castelsagrat after crossing the Garonne and raided towards Agen. Baldwin Botetourt (master of the prince's great horses) was based at Brassac. The first six weeks of 1356 was scarcely less damaging to French royal interests in the south than the *grande chevauchée* itself and perhaps in strategic terms they were more significant. Territorial gains were modest but important due to their concentration in the north-west march and the newfound, if unreliable, Plantagenet allies brought further territorial control. Durfort controlled some thirty walled towns, Caumont a further six and Galard and Albret were highly significant landholders. More than this, 'They were the weather-vanes of the south-west',[10] their allegiance marked the ascendancy of the English and the prince; similarly their defection in 1368–69 would mark his decline.

3

THE CAMPAIGN OF 1356

The success of the first raid and the support of new allies and the despatch of reinforcements demanded a succeeding campaign. Further troops led by some distinguished figures sailed from England. Letters of protection were made out for Edward le Despenser (Lord le Despenser from 1357), William 3rd Lord Morley, Edward Courtenay (the prince's bachelor and retainer and member of the house of the earl of Devon) and 119 others going to join the retinues of the prince and his captains on 28 March 1356. The 1356 campaign was to be fought under different conditions, however, as on 12 January Edward III had given the prince authority to undertake peace negotiations with the French. The new raid was once again part of a wider strategic programme involving Lancaster and the intention seems to have been that they were to join forces. In retrospect, problems of communication and the pressure and limited opportunities created by the French defenders meant that if such co-ordination was achieved it would be more by luck than judgement. Lancaster invaded Normandy in June and was joined by Robert Knolles, Jean de Montfort, Philip of Navarre and Godfrey de Harcourt. They departed on 22 June, re-supplied the Navarrese strongholds of Pont-Audemar and Breteuil, avoided battle and

9. Great Seal of Edward III.

diverted attention from the south. On 8 August, Lancaster was commissioned to begin a campaign in Penthièvre.[1]

The reason given for the expedition was that the prince wished to face the count of Poitiers, now the king's lieutenant in Languedoc, who was believed to be at Bourges and had been gathering troops since mid-May. Troops assembled there in June and July led by Jean de Clermont, Jean le Maingre, the seneschals of Poitou, Saintonge and Toulouse and the royal secretary, Pierre de Labatut.[2] In the prince's absence, Gascony was again not to be left undefended, particularly as the English had received intelligence that Armagnac was likely to attack after the departure of the expeditionary force. John Chivereston, the seneschal of the duchy, Bernard d'Albret and Thomas Roos, mayor of Bordeaux, remained behind in command of the defence.

The prince left Bergerac, to where he had moved his operational headquarters, in early August with an army numbering 6,000–7,000 troops. Despite Stafford's efforts, this was probably not as large a force as the prince would have wished. He had to

deal with problems of desertion – orders were sent to the lieu-
tenant-justice of Cheshire regarding forty-three deserters – and
some other troops were given a formal leave of absence such as
William Jodrell who received the famous Jodrell deed. His
brother, John, fought at Poitiers as part of a company of bowmen
raised from among the burgesses and inhabitants of Llantrisant.[3]

Those that remained marched north along the east of the
Massif Central through Périgord, the Limousin and Poitou. The
second raid was not characterised, at least by the chroniclers, as
being as destructive as that of 1355, but this is not to say that the
Agenais, the Limousin and La Marche escaped without harm.
After crossing the Vienne there was some inconclusive skirmishing outside Bourges, which, although the count of Poitiers
was not present, was heavily fortified and remained strongly
defended. Unsurprisingly, the force attracted attention almost
from the outset.

Since 12 July, King Jean II had been laying siege to the castle
of Breteuil, a Navarrese stronghold in eastern Normandy. It was
well-supplied and vigorously defended and the French royal army
made little headway. The costs of French military action were
becoming crippling and news that yet another English army was
being prepared resulted in a drastic devaluation of the coinage.
The time and expense of the siege of Breteuil, not to mention
the king's personal reputation, meant that failure was not an
option. Consequently, when Jean realised that the siege would
not be concluded militarily and that his troops were needed
urgently in the south to counter the threat of the Black Prince,
he paid the Navaresse an enormous sum to abandon the castle
with the promise of free passage to rejoin Philippe of Navarre in
the Contentin. The king reorganised his forces at Chartres, doing
away with much of his infantry, realising that he had to counter
the mobility of the Anglo-Gascon army. There he was joined by
William Douglas and troops from Scotland, but the response from
the French nobility was disappointing.

The French army had not undergone the same transformation
with regard to its methods of recruitment and implementation of
strategy as the English, although advances had been made in both
areas. By c.1350, possibly as a consequence of the English expedition of 1346–47, the French monarchy did not recruit many

troops on the basis of the traditional feudal array, except when land was held on the annuity known as the *fief-rente*. Verbal or written contracts were common. However, Jean II still made extensive use of the traditional call for military service for mounted troops, the *ban* and the *arrière-ban*. These different forms of recruitment provided the French monarchy with substantial armies if not as large as Philippe VI brought to Crécy.[4]

The prince's army headed for the French interior and Edward spent the night at Vierzon, which he burned on leaving. Scouting parties made contact with French forces and Chandos and Audley encountered a French detachment led by Philippe de Chambly who had been dispatched by Jean to delay the prince and allow the king time to bring his own forces into effect. On about 28 August, the prince learned that Jean's army was at Orléans and had not yet joined the count of Poitiers. The army advanced along the valley of the Cher to Romorantin, which capitulated on 30 August although the keep of the castle held out for another three days when Marshal Boucicaut and Amaury, sire de Craon, were captured. They had been sent to obstruct the prince and slow his advance and in this at least they succeeded. The delay caused by the siege gave the French royal army an opportunity to eat into the Anglo-Gascon lead. As had happened in 1346, relatively small gains were given precedence over the potentially disastrous consequences that could result from the time lost to acquire them. That is unless the English either in 1346 or 1356 or both were deliberately trying to provoke a French attack.[5]

The raiders marched westwards towards Tours down the bank of the Cher but were unable to cross the Loire, near Amboise, thereby precluding any meeting with Lancaster. The French had broken every bridge over the river between Tours and Blois. The prince was hoping for support and was 'intending to meet our dear cousin... of whom we heard for certain that he was trying to march towards us.'[6] Lacking supplies and ever more aware of the approach of the French army, the prince found himself resting for four days near Tours after a march of 320 miles in thirty-two days. The French royal army had moved more swiftly but in doing so had become extended over a considerable distance. On about 10 September, Jean joined forces with the

10. Seal of Edward, prince of Aquitaine.

count of Poitiers and crossed the Loire at Blois before marching towards Amboise only some ten miles from the prince's army. The threat was now that the English might be caught between the king and Clermont who had been sent to organise the defence of Touraine. Edward withdrew over the Rivers Cher and Indre. On Monday 12 September, it became clear that a battle was becoming very likely and the papacy took a hand to try and prevent bloodshed. Cardinal Talleyrand de Périgord attempted to broker a truce but failed. The negotiations also slowed the progress of the army and only twelve miles were covered that day. After reaching Montbazan on 18 September, the prince's scouts found the French army outside Poitiers. Attempts were made again by Cardinal Talleyrand to make peace and the prince appeared willing to make a number of concessions including the forfeiture of all that had been gained in the campaign including property and prisoners and an oath not to take up arms against the king of France for seven years. This may have been as much due to his fear of being holed up and starved out than it was of engaging the enemy. It was also a Sunday and the Cardinal argued that the truce of God should be observed at least until sunrise of the following day. The delay that this produced meant both that the French had time to bring in reinforcements and that the English could entrench their position and build defensive screens for the archers. The French negotiators included Charny and the archbishop of Sens and the English were represented by Warwick, Suffolk, Burghersh, Chandos and Audley. However, the French insistence on total surrender was refused. Charny proposed a duel between a hundred troops from both sides but this also was rejected.

The battle lines were drawn on broken ground on the plains of Maupertuis.[7] The battlefield was situated some 8 km to the south-east of Poitiers, and to the north and the west of the wood of Nouaillé on an incline near the River Miosson.

4

THE BATTLE OF POITIERS

On the morning of the battle (19 September), the sun rose a little before 6 o'clock and the day promised to be warm and clear. Cardinal Talleyrand made a final visit to the English camp in the hope of preventing a confrontation. Once more, the prince appears to have been willing to seek a compromise but his terms were again rejected by King Jean. After Talleyrand departed and made for Poitiers it was clear that a battle could not be avoided.

The assault does not appear to have been launched immediately as there was some disagreement in the French ranks as to the best plan of attack. One reason for this may have been the strength of the defensive position that the Anglo-Gascon army occupied, this certainly was one of the main reasons given for the failure of the eventual French assault by the author of the *Chronique des règnes de Jean II et Charles V*.[1]

There is some disagreement about whether the English forces were retreating before battle was joined. The delay caused by Talleyrand's attempts to broker a truce may have offered the prince an opportunity to escape and he may have been trying to get away right up until the moment of the French attack. Following the decision of a council held the previous evening, the earl of Warwick led his forces and perhaps the baggage-train near the marshes to the south of the Champ d'Alexandre and over or towards the ford across the River Miosson. The prince described the plan as follows:

> Because we were short of supplies and for other reasons, it was agreed that we should retreat in a flanking movement, so that if they wanted to attack or to approach us in a position which was not in any way greatly to our disadvantage we would give battle.[2]

This was written after the event but does not indicate that the prince was looking for a battle at that time, nor did he feel the need to hide the fact that retreat was part of his plan. It is unclear if the prince intended to retreat as early as possible or only if the attack proved to be too strong. It is possible however, that it may have been a feint to provoke a French attack. If so, it succeeded.

According to what was now normal English practice, the prince had laid out his army in three battles and had taken what advantage he could of the terrain. The location of the battle of Poitiers is highly conjectural and, as the terrain played an important part, this is an extremely significant issue and one that cannot be completely resolved. It is clear that Jean caught the prince south of Poitiers on the banks of the River Miosson. Edward, it appears, was able to draw his force to an area of broken ground uncharacteristic of the plains of the area. Three divisions defended a position protected by natural obstacles, hedges, trees and marshy areas that allowed the French only two routes of attack. It seems likely that the English army was drawn up behind a hawthorn hedge through which there were two substantial gaps (enough for four men to ride abreast, according to Froissart). There was a brief slope falling away in front of them and then the ground began to rise towards the French. This meant that the French could charge downhill most of the way to the English lines but the last few metres were uphill as well as being well protected by the hedge and other defensive contrivances. The gaps in the hedge were protected by archers so that any French troops that attempted to break through would have to run the gauntlet of a hail of arrows. In the first phase of the battle, the difficult terrain and the impact of the archers

11. Jupon with the arms of Edward the Black Prince. Part of his funeral 'achievements' above his tomb in Canterbury Cathedral.

proved to be a match for the cavalry charges led against the English lines by the French marshals, Jean de Clermont and Arnoul d'Audrehem.

The three Anglo-Gascon battles were each led by a seasoned commander. The first battle, the vanguard (located, somewhat confusingly, in the southernmost position), was under the orders of the earl of Warwick, accompanied by the earl of Oxford, the captal de Buch, the lord of Pommiers and several other Gascon barons. The prince took charge personally at the head of the second battle, and he surrounded himself with experienced soldiers such as John Chandos, James Audley, Reginald Cobham and Bartholomew Burghersh. The earls of Salisbury and Suffolk controlled the third battle, the rear-guard, composed of one of the main archer corps and including some German troops. This defended the most significant breach in the hedge.

The French army was drawn up in four battles and was situated some distance from the English, out of bowshot, perhaps 500–600 metres away. That part of the French vanguard which was commanded by the constable, Gautier de Brienne, the exiled duke of Athens, was on foot and the marshals, Audrehem and Clermont, led a shock cavalry force to test and distract the English archers while the other battles advanced on foot. Among the ranks of the vanguard were such soldiers as the lords of Aubigny and Ribemont and a German contingent under the leadership of the counts of Sarrebruck, Nassau and Nidau. Of the three other units, one was under the king's brother, the duke of Orléans, and the second was, if only nominally, commanded by the dauphin Charles, duke of Normandy. He was still only a teenager, and the king had reinforced this battle and assigned experienced soldiers to it, such as the duke of Bourbon, the lords of Saint-Venant and Landas, and Thomas de Voudenay; Tristan de Maignelay was the ducal standard-bearer. The king directed the last French battle which included a number of his close relations, such as his youngest son, Philippe, and the counts de Ponthieu, Eu, Longueville, Sancerre and Dammartin. Geoffroy de Charny carried the royal banner, the Oriflamme. The bulk of the French army was dismounted in an attempt to counter the English tactics that had proved so successful at Crécy, and following the advice of the Scottish knight Sir

William Douglas, who had brought 200 men-at-arms to serve King Jean.

PHASE ONE

The examples of the encounters at Courtrai, Bannockburn and, to a lesser extent, Crécy should have guided the French military command. Discipline, order and close communication were vital elements in launching an assault against an infantry enemy supported by archers in a well-defended position. In the event the initial charge was presumptuous, premature and poorly co-ordinated. After the departure of the papal legate to the safety of Poitiers, the command of the French vanguard became divided between Audrehem and Clermont who are reported to have argued over the best course of action, one recommending patience, the other making accusations of cowardice. This dispute had been prompted when they became aware that the earl of Warwick was leading his men and some of the baggage-train away from the field. It is questionable whether this was a pretence to encourage the French to attack, or a real attempt to withdraw. The cavalry unit divided and Audrehem led his men to engage the prince's forces at the bottom of the hill while Clermont, perhaps after a short delay, rode against the English at the western edge of the wood. The assault by the marshals brought Warwick back into the fray and he re-crossed the Miosson at the Gué de l'homme and engaged Audrehem's forces. In this he may have been supported by a detachment of archers from the earl of Oxford's men located on the edge of the marsh. This was successful, mainly because the archers were able to shoot at the flanks and rumps of the horses which were unprotected and Warwick was able to re-order his archers on the flank of the prince's division. Meanwhile or perhaps a little later, Clermont and the constable charged against the battle led by Salisbury, which was on the opposite wing at the north-western edge of the wood of Nouaillé. Salisbury's archers fired on Clermont's men as they approached and then the infantry moved to block their approach through one of the gaps in the hedge. The earl of Suffolk encouraged the defence and brought up reinforcements to withstand the attack and the French were driven back; both Clermont and Brienne were killed. On the other flank Audrehem was captured, and Douglas badly wounded. Although it was by no means apparent at this point, the failure of the French vanguard to break the ranks of the English archers proved to be decisive. Geoffrey Le Baker indicates that the power of the longbow at relatively short distance was devastating, and, if the angle of impact was correct, the arrows would punch through the French armour.[3]

PHASE TWO

The dauphin's division followed the French vanguard into battle and marched to engage the dismounted Anglo-Gascons and managed to do so despite the onslaught of the English archers. The French forces in this battle probably numbered about 4,000 and this part of the engagement may have lasted as long as two hours. The assault was impeded by the retreating vanguard which disrupted their approach and this was compounded by the work of the English longbowmen who caused a great deal of destruction as the French tried to break through the hedge. Nonetheless, the dauphin and the duke of Bourbon, who fell in the conflict, led their troops to the English lines and a keenly fought struggle ensued. The French were only finally thrown back after heavy casualties were sustained on both sides and the dauphin's standard-bearer was taken captive. The battle was once more thrown into the balance and it is possible that if King Jean had attacked at once with his remaining forces that the outcome might have been different. Instead he took a more prudent course and dismissed his three elder sons, including the dauphin, from the field. In addition to weakening the numbers at his disposal, this also seems to have caused a loss of morale among many of the remaining French troops. This may have caused the division under the command of the young duke of Orléans to flee towards Chauvigny or it may be that Orléans was also commanded to retreat. In any case, 'from the moment this large body of troops turned away from the fight a French victory became almost impossible.'[4]

The withdrawal of some of the French army gave the English a moment's respite to re-gather, re-arm themselves with those few arrows that they could collect and to deal with their casualties. Some in the prince's battle apparently thought that the entire French host had withdrawn and launched an attack in the hope of taking prisoners. The earl of Warwick may have been among them. Maurice Berkeley was certainly one of these. He was of course, mistaken and acquired the unfortunate distinction of being one of very few Englishmen taken captive at Poitiers. He was captured by a Picard knight named Jean d'Ellenes.

Phase Three

The remaining French troops joined with the battle commanded by King Jean and slowly advanced giving the Anglo-Gascons more time to recover. This was a substantial force and included a large number of crossbowmen who may have originally been part of the constable's division. These indulged in a long-range exchange with the English archers which had little effect on either side. On this occasion, the archers did not make much impact on the main body of the French infantry when it came into range. This was due to a lack of arrows on the English side meaning they did not have sufficient ammunition to maintain the barrage and the French approach under cover of an interlinked shield-wall. While effective, this tactic delayed the French advance and accounts for the slowness with which they approached. The majority of this part of the French army was still fresh and had not been involved in any fighting while the English had been engaged in the conflict, albeit with brief intermissions for up to three hours.

In response, the Black Prince re-ordered his forces, drawing them together in a single division, by this point the English forces probably outnumbered the remainder of the French army. He also took the tactical initiative by having some of his men-at-arms remount their horses and prepare to charge the French lines. Secondly, he gave the command to the captal de Buch to lead a cavalry detachment in an encircling manoeuvre by which they would be concealed from the French behind a small hill. The longbowmen fired their remaining arrows, although with little effect it seems and then joined the infantry, fighting with daggers and swords. The prince possibly also remounted another contingent of men from his division who attacked the French. This group may have included James Audley. Once the captal's men, numbering some sixty men-at-arms and 100 mounted archers, were in position, they and the combined forces of the English division and the remaining cavalry coincided their attacks. This final phase of the battle was again a close run affair, but the assault on two flanks ultimately proved successful. The English victory may also have been aided by the return of a number of troops, possibly led by the earl of Warwick who had detached in the pursuit of prisoners earlier in the engagement.

It is somewhat ironic that the results of the defeat at Poitiers might have been lessened if the battle had not been so closely fought. If the outcome had been apparent much earlier in the day the king and many of his high-ranking nobles who were killed or taken prisoner would have had time to retreat. One of the final indications of French defeat was the fall of the standard-bearer, Geoffrey de Charny, 'the most worthy and valiant of them all' according to Froissart, who was killed with the Oriflamme in his hand.[5] Jean himself was finally overwhelmed in the crush of men. He was in considerable danger after he surrendered as many men jostled to be the one who took him and his son Philippe. First, Denis de Morbeke, a knight of Artois, took the king who gave him one of his gauntlets to indicate his surrender. However, a number of others, mainly Gascons led by a squire called Bernard de Troys, then grabbed hold of Jean. Further danger and indignity was forestalled by the arrival of Reginald Cobham and the earl of Warwick on horseback who forced back the struggling crowd and guided the king and what remained of his entourage to safety.

With the king taken, the battle was finished, and the chase for the remaining prisoners began. Some of the French were routed into the marshes below the original English position and those others that could, fled towards Poitiers 8 km to the north-west of the battlefield. Englishmen and Gascons pursued them to the walls, which forced the townsmen to close the gates for the defence of the city. A terrible massacre followed under the walls, and many Frenchmen readily opted for captivity in order to save their own lives.

While French casualties and captives were very considerable – 2,500 men-at-arms – the number of Anglo-Gascons who were killed was comparatively small. Only forty men-at-arms were recorded as being slain in addition to an undisclosed (and presumably much more sizeable) number of infantry and archers. Many more were wounded. One William Lenche lost an eye in the battle and the prince rewarded him with the rights to the ferry in Saltash. James Audley was also gravely wounded, in recognition of which he was granted the most generous annuity of all those awarded as a consequence of service to the prince in 1355–56, £400.

With considerations of strategy completed and the battle won, the prince invited all the captured nobles to dine with him.

> The prince himself served the king's table, and all the other tables as well with every mark of humility, and refused to sit at the king's table saying he was not yet worthy of such an honour, and that it would not be fitting for him to sit at the same table as so great a prince, and one who had shown himself so valiant that day.[6]

Such courteous behaviour set the seal on what was to become the almost legendary reputation of the Black Prince but it was courtesy and a chivalric attitude that was employed after the battle had been won, it was courtesy to those of noble and royal blood and of course, it was courtesy to a relative.

The victory at Poitiers and the capture of Jean changed the diplomatic and political balance of Anglo-French relations but to what extent and how far would be the subject of hard bargaining. Geoffrey Hamelyn, the prince's attendant, was sent to London with Jean's tunic and helmet as proof of his capture. The army returned to Bordeaux and negotiations began regarding a truce and the exact price of a king's ransom.

ANALYSIS OF THE BATTLE

The sources for the battle of Poitiers are difficult, often contradictory and lacking detail. They include chronicles and campaign letters which need to be used in conjunction with cartographic evidence although with the understanding that natural features may not be identical to those in 1356. In particular the extent of marshland around the Miosson and the size of the wood of Nouaillé must be conjectural. More significantly for the purposes of reconstructing the initial disposition of troops the length and position of the hedge and ditches which protected the Anglo-Gascon position is especially problematic. There have been many attempts to describe the battle and many of these have been consulted alongside a range of contemporary and near-contemporary sources. Any reconstruction must be hypothetical due to the nature of those sources and not all the issues have been resolved satisfactorily. The key problem lies in the initial disposition of English and French forces after which the course of the battle is somewhat more straightforward. The battle plans provide an interpretation of the encounter but some evidence will be cited at length so that the reader may come to his or her own conclusions.[7]

A number of campaign letters were written concerning the engagement but most of these such as Burghersh's dispatch which was recorded by Froissart, merely noted the names and number of casualties and prisoners taken and that the battle took place half a league from Poitiers. The prince himself wrote to the mayor, commons and aldermen of London on 22 October and provides no information concerning the disposition of troops, merely noting that 'our very dear and beloved knight Nigel Loryng, our chamberlain, who is bringing this [letter], will tell you more in detail from his own knowledge.'[8] The situation prior to the battle is best described by the Anonimalle Chronicler.

That night [Saturday, 17 September 1356] the prince encamped with all his army in a wood on a little river near the site of the defeat... On Monday morning... the Earl of Warwick crossed a narrow causeway over the marsh... but the press of the carriage of the English army was so great and the causeway so narrow that they could hardly pass and so they remained up through the first hour of daylight. And then they saw the vanguard of the French come towards the Prince... And so the Earl of Warwick turned back with his men...[9]

It appears that some of inherent contradiction in the sources can be resolved if the events they describe are considered to have been contracted or expanded over time. Such an interpretation should be considered when reading Le Baker's account below. This provides an explanation for the positioning of the prince in a more northerly location along the wood. He first camped around the south and then moved north, perhaps making a camp on the hill to the north of the wood. From there his forces were repositioned along the western edge of the wood protected by the hedge that may have run along much of the length of the road. The gaps described may have been made by the carters mentioned.

One of the most useful sources for the battle is the chronicle written by Geoffrey Le Baker. He states that:

> ...he [the prince] surveyed the scene, and saw that to one side there was a nearby hill... Between our men and the hill was a broad deep valley and marsh watered by a stream. The prince's battalion crossed the stream at a fairly narrow ford and occupied the hill beyond the marshes and ditches where they easily concealed their positions among the thickets, lying higher than the enemy. The field in which our vanguard and centre were stationed was separated from the level ground which the French occupied by a long hedge and ditch, whose other end reached down to the marsh. The earl of Warwick in command of the vanguard, held the slope down to the marsh. In the upper part of the hedge, well away from the slope, there was a certain open space or gap, made by the carters in autumn, a stone's throw away from which our rearguard was positioned, under the command of the earl of Salisbury.[10]

Some further details are provided by the less than reliable Jean Froissart, but his testimony cannot be ignored.

'And how are they disposed?' asked the King. 'Sire', replied Sir Eustace [de Ribemont], 'they are in a very strong position... They have chosen a length of road strongly protected by hedges and bushes and they have lined the hedge on both sides with their archers, so that one cannot enter that road or ride along it without passing between them. Yet one must go that way before one can fight them... At the end of the hedge, among vines and thorn-bushes between which it would be impossible to march or ride, are their men-at-arms... It is a very skilful piece of work.'[11]

This fairly detailed description is also confusing. Froissart suggests that the Anglo-Gascons were arranged along a road which was strongly protected by hedges, an approach I have followed. His comment that these were lined with archers so that any assault had to pass between them requires some assumptions about the positioning of a gap and therefore the disposition of the archers. This gap was only wide enough for four men to ride abreast. It's presumed, if one accepts this account, that the archers were drawn up behind a hedge facing the French and this hedge was bisected with a road and/or the carters' track. There were also archers at either end of the hedge arranged in a formation that Froissart describes as being in the form of a 'herce', possibly a triangle or 'harrow' shape. This can be explained by the archers under Salisbury to the north and those commanded by Warwick to the south.

One of the reasons for the prince's success in 1356 and indeed of the English during this phase of the Hundred Years War was the composition of the armies that encountered the French. This developed from the salutary lessons the English had received at the hands of the Scots from the early years of the fourteenth century. The war that the English fought in France was a mobile one that struck at the social and economic foundations of the Valois kingdom and yet allowed for the possibility of a set-piece encounter. The evolution, if not revolution, in military thinking that had occurred since the reign of Edward I resulted in an increasingly professional army, one which was recruited to perform a specific task. Troops were recruited after 1347 almost entirely through the indenture system by which captains signed up to lead a particular number of soldiers armed to particular specifications to implement a range of strategic and tactical plans. The prince's forces at Poitiers and during the *chevauchées* of 1355 and 1356 consisted of three types of troops – men-at-arms, horsed archers and footmen. This allowed for an extremely flexible tactical response to a variety of situations.

The Anglo-Gascon army was probably composed of 3,000–4,000 men-at-arms, 2,500–3,000 archers and 1,000 other light troops. The French army may have included 8,000 men-at-arms, 2,000 *arbalesters* and numerous other poorly trained and lightly armed troops totalling some 15,000–16,000.

Jean could raise fewer men for Poitiers than his father had ten years before although contemporaries did not attribute defeat to a shortage of manpower. Rather, and particularly by the author of *La complainte sur la bataille de Poitiers*, blame was heaped upon the nobility.[12] The purpose of the aristocracy was military; the traditional *raison d'être* of the nobility, the reasoning which underpinned its pre-eminent social position, was that its members fought in the defence of the land. They were, in traditional feudal parlance, the *bellatores* – those who fought – and if they failed in this role, they failed in their primary function and duty. It is significant that the revolt of the Jacquerie which occurred in the anarchy and power-vacuum after Poitiers was focused against the French aristocracy and not, in the main, due to economic and social impositions. It was an assault on the general failure of the nobility to fulfil its traditional role. Added to the failure of French chivalry were other more prosaic reasons for the defeat, one of which was the inferiority of the crossbow and the comparatively few of them which Jean had at his disposal. Crossbows could do considerable damage but they were slow and clumsy weapons compared to the longbow. Furthermore, the English had been allowed time to prepare their position. They were well dug-in behind earthworks and the natural protection of the hedge and wood and with the terrain in their favour. 'Par son recrutement, et plus encore par sa préparation immédiate, la petite armée du prince de Galles était dans les meilleures conditions pour vaincre.'[13]

The English were drawn up in three major battles. The Anglo-Gascon vanguard was led by Warwick, Oxford and the captal de Buch, and the rearguard by Salisbury and Suffolk. The bulk of the prince's retinue was in the centre led by Edward, with Burghersh, Audley, Chandos and Cobham. The archers were stationed on the flanks and possibly at right angles to the enemy due to the nature of the 'herce' formation (on the battle plans depicted as a 'harrow'). Their positions may have been defended with earthworks. The French divisions attacked in turn not *en masse*, and Orléans fled or was dismissed before engaging the enemy.

One important aspect of the battle was its length, it lasted considerably longer than most medieval engagements. As at Crécy, the longbowmen proved extremely effective against mounted troops, but were to prove less so against infantry advancing in close formation, that is until the French were at close range when the longbows with their heavy draw-weights could punch through French armour. The length of the battle meant that arrows were in short supply after the opening salvos. The French army was in its entirety considerably larger than the Anglo-Gascon force, perhaps twice its size but that weight of numbers was not brought together at one time and in many of the phases of the battle the prince may not have been at any sort of numerical disadvantage.

The victory at Poitiers combined the defensive tactics, demonstrated and witnessed by the prince at Crécy, with the chivalric traditions of an earlier age. Only the French vanguard, led by the marshals, was mounted. After the failure of the French attacks, part of the Anglo-Gascon response was the classic heavy cavalry charge. To add a more modern flavour to this tradition, the flanking force led by the captal de Buch may have included mounted archers and possibly Gascon cross-bowmen. The battle was thus a fine illustration of the use of dismounted troops who, as at Crécy, in concert with archers in a defensible position, broke the French attacks, then remounted and were victorious by the use of a cavalry attack, which was now uncommon, if not anachronistic.

It is uncertain whether a set-piece battle was ever intended at least under the conditions in which the prince found himself not far from Poitiers. If a meeting with Lancaster had been achieved then the combined force would have been strengthened to such an extent that a successful battle might have seemed likely. Certainly, Crécy provided a precedent. Had additional forces and resources been available, and the arrival of the Black Death not precluded further military action, then the 1346–47 campaign and the victory at Crécy might well have yielded far greater spoils than Calais and the ransoms of a few and deaths of many of the French nobility. It seems extremely likely that the prince was seeking a battle in 1355 and 1356, but he was seeking a battle on his own terms and with an enemy against whom he felt confident of victory. The concessions that the prince was willing to make prior to the battle and some of his remarks made afterwards suggest that he was not terribly confident early on the morning of Monday 19 September. The victory at Poitiers altered and reinforced English strategic thinking. They had demonstrated in Scotland and in France that if they could bring an enemy to battle on their own terms then they could win: that confidence probably also coloured wider aspirations in the Hundred Years War. The struggle which previously had been about obtaining sovereign rule in Gascony fought under the flag, almost the excuse of the English claim to the throne of France, became, albeit briefly, a fight for that throne.

After the defeat at Crécy, the French had made several attempts to combat the English particularly through imitating their tactics and dismounting their own men-at-arms for example at the battles of Lunalonge (Poitou, 1349), Taillebourg (near Saintes, 8 April 1351), Ardres (6 June 1351) and Mauron (14 August 1352). The example of battles such as Courtrai (1302), Morgarten (1315) and Crécy had also affected French military thinking and they endeavoured to find a weakness in the infantry-archer formation. In the event these approaches proved ineffective or were not put into action at Poitiers. The use of a mounted force to lead the attack was one such innovation but the defeat at Poitiers destroyed the illusion that French military changes could be effective at least until the advent of practical artillery. The contrast between the French response in 1356 and that of 1359 is very clear. It was such defensive tactics that allowed them to turn the tables on the English, first by denying Edward the crown in

1359–60 and then by reversing the territorial gains that the English had gained through the treaty of Brétigny. This was only possible when they had an easily assailable military objective, the principality of Aquitaine.

ARCHERS AND THE LONGBOW

The role of the longbow in the early campaigns of the Hundred Years War is a contentious matter. A number of issues are open to argument and interpretation, ranging from the nature of the weapons themselves, their power and rate of accurate fire, to the disposition of the archers on the battlefield. In part, the trouble lies in the fact that there are no extant medieval longbows. The earliest examples are those excavated from the wreck of the Mary Rose. If these were finished longbows representative of those used at Poitiers then they were extremely potent weapons with an effective range of 300 metres or more. By contrast, the wooden or composite crossbows of the time could shoot about 200 metres and for every two quarrels, a bowman might fire up to twenty arrows. Thus, well-trained longbowmen with a sufficient supply of arrows could, if this is an accurate picture, cause a great deal of damage and disruption to an enemy attack. What is not in doubt is that archers became an increasingly important component in English armies in the course of the Hundred Years War. The proportion of longbowmen to other troops was regularly 3, 4 or 5:1 and sometimes reached as high as 20:1. However, the 'invincibility' of the longbow has been questioned in recent years. It is argued that, rather than causing a great number of casualties, archer fire caused the enemy either to be 'funnelled' into a particular area where the English infantry defences were at their strongest or simply to disrupt the assault so that they did not prove as great a threat.

Longbowmen alone did not win the battle of Poitiers (or those of Crécy and Agincourt) but they were a critical component of the armies that secured those victories. When working with infantry and a final cavalry charge to rout the enemy they proved, whether through the number of casualties that they inflicted or through the sheer scale of the disruption

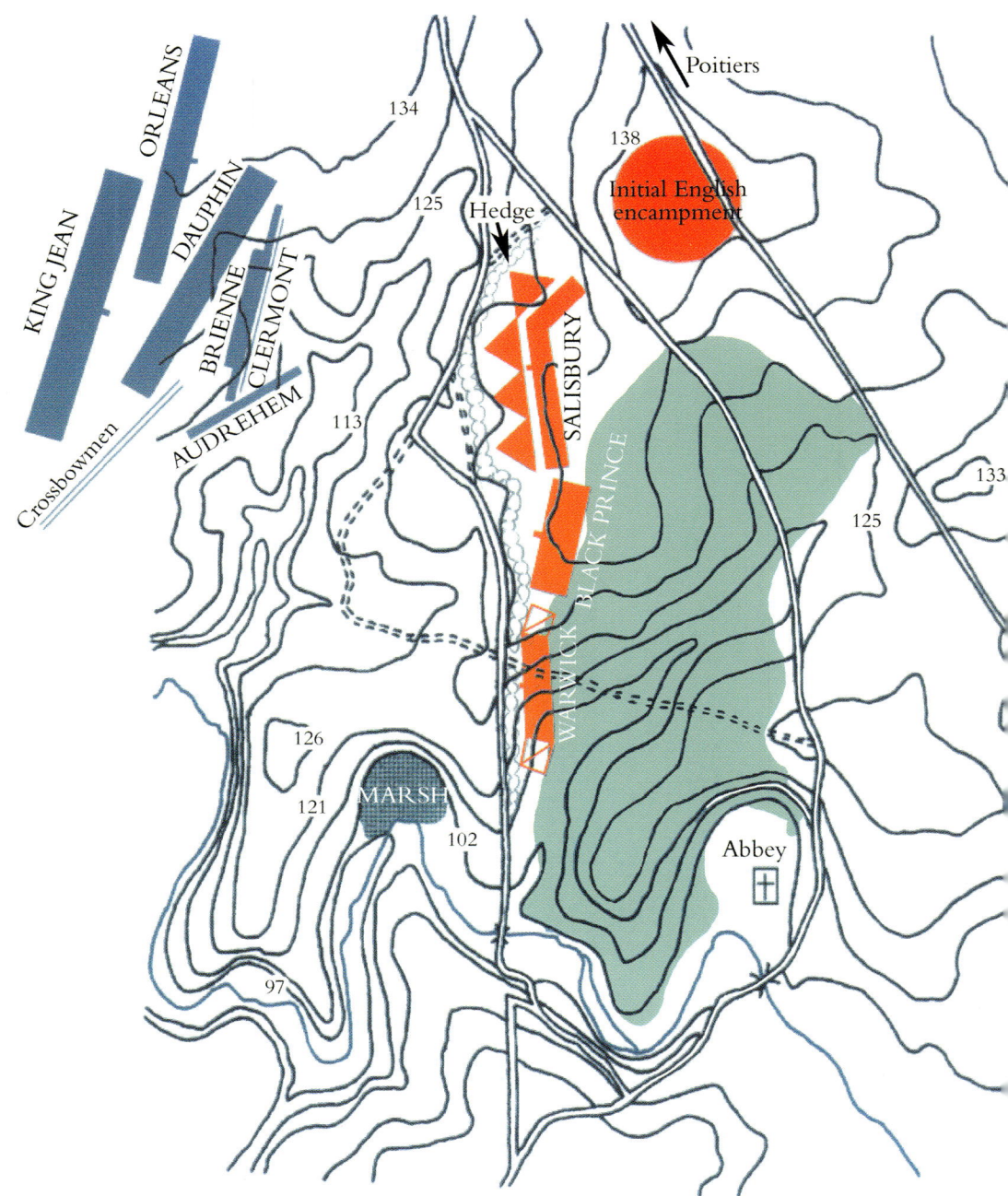

ORLEANS

KING JEAN

DAUPHIN

BRIENNE

CLERMONT

AUDREHEM

Crossbowmen

134

125

Hedge

Poitiers

138

Initial English encampment

SALISBURY

113

133

125

BLACK PRINCE

WARWICK

126

121

MARSH

102

97

Abbey

2. Sunday – Initial Dispositions. French: Audrehem, Clermont and Brienne drawn up together in advance of the Dauphin. English: Warwick defensively aligned at this stage behind the hedge and on/in the fringes of the wood. Warwick's route with the baggage train on Monday morning (early) is uncertain. There may well have been passable tracks through Nouaillé Wood.

Previous page 1. Tomb of the Black Prince, Canterbury cathedral.

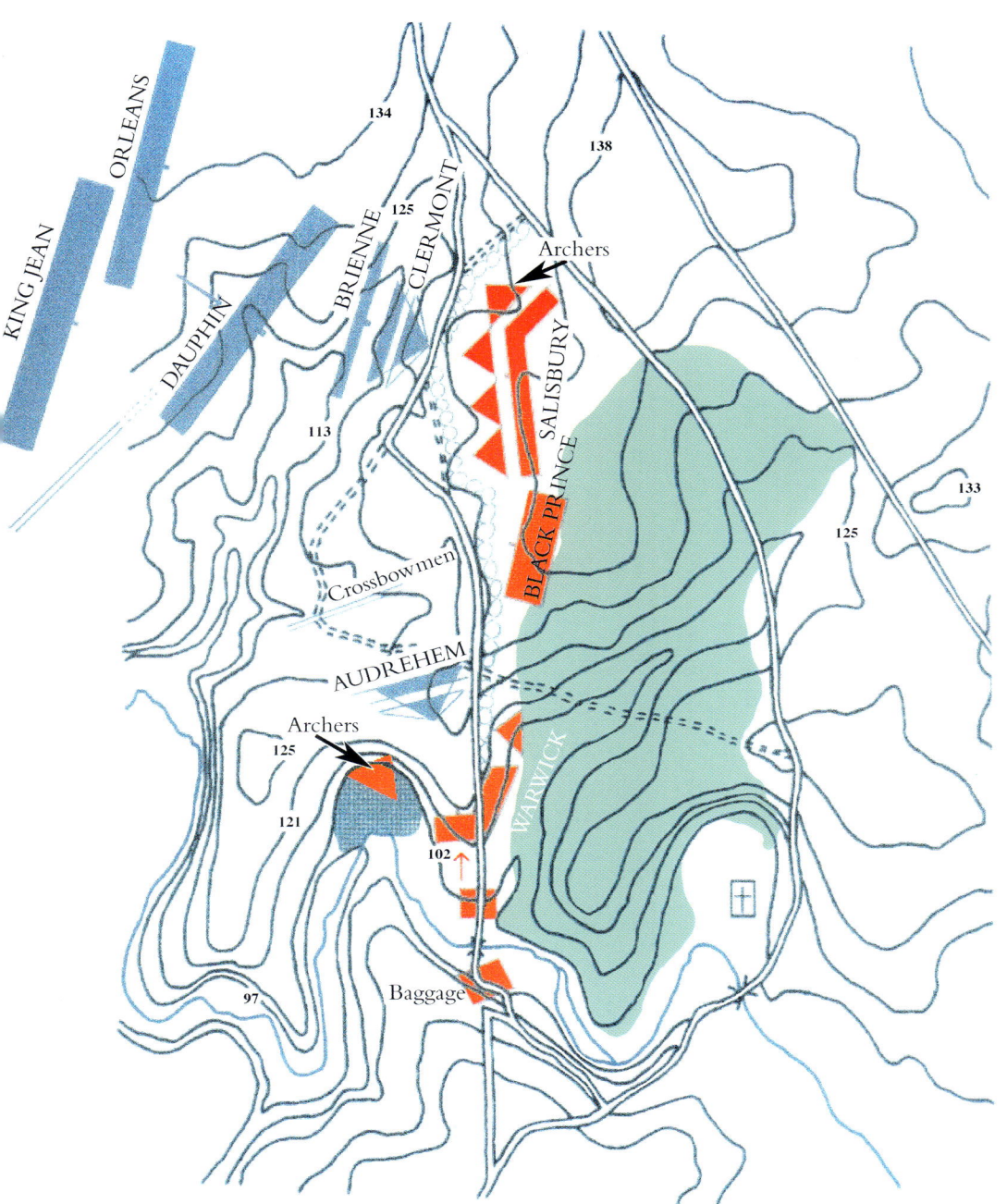

KING JEAN

ORLEANS

DAUPHIN

BRIENNE

CLERMONT

134

138

125

Archers

SALISBURY

113

BLACK PRINCE

133

125

Crossbowmen

AUDREHEM

Archers

125

WARWICK

121

102

97

Baggage

3. The Attack of the Marshals. French: i) Audrehem rides south, encounters Warwick and detachment of archers. ii) Clemont and Brienne assualt Anglo-Gascon rearguard commanded by Salisbury. English: i) Warwick returns to counter Audrehem. ii) Archers deployed to disrupt French attacks.

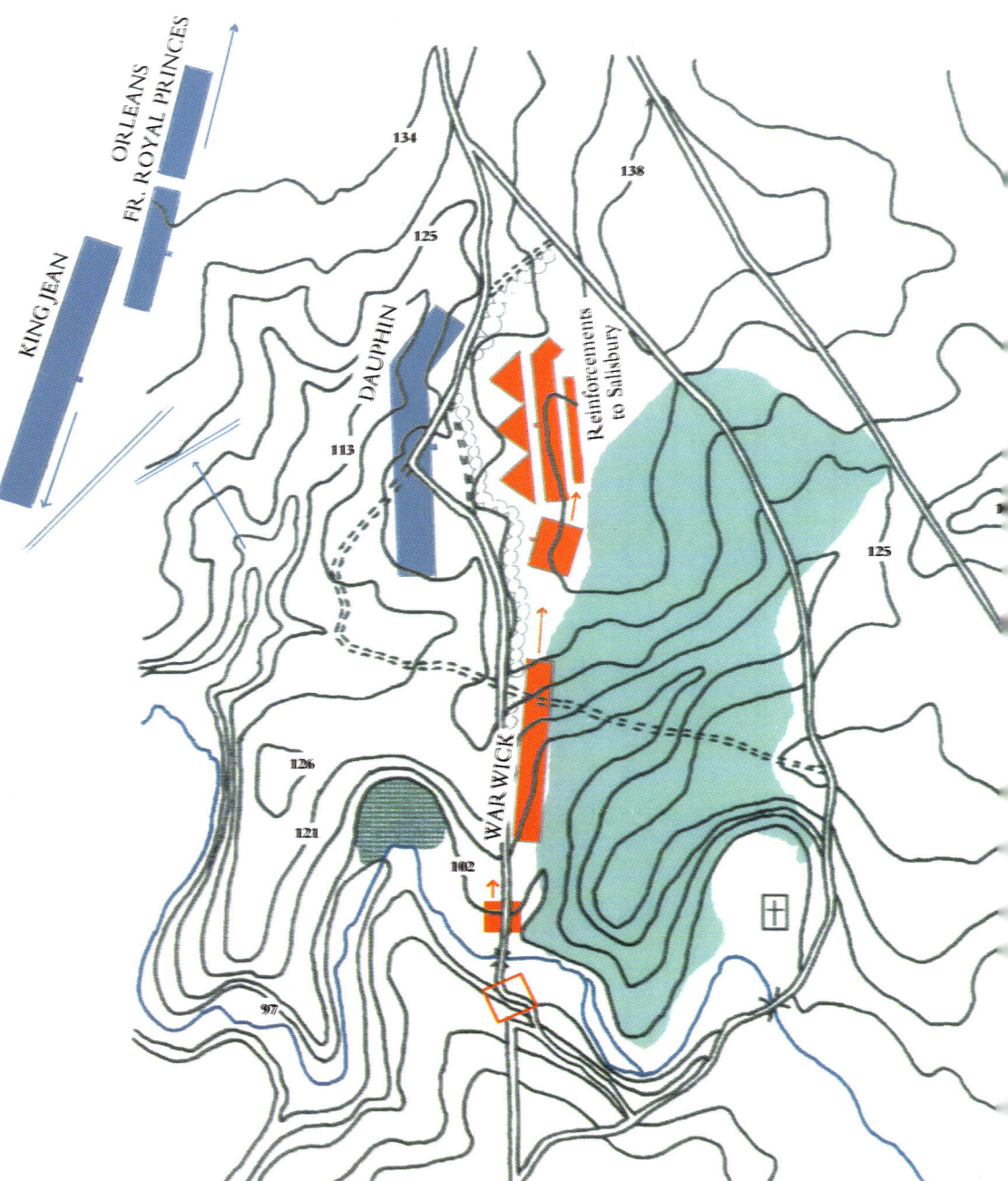

ORLEANS
FR. ROYAL PRINCES
KING JEAN
134
138
125
DAUPHIN
113
Reinforcements to Salisbury
125
126
WARWICK
121
102
97

4. The Dauphin's Attack. French: i) Dauphin's attack faltering; ii) French royal princes ordered from the battlefield; iii) Orléans and *some* of his forces leave the battlefield; iv) King Jean's force moves further south. English: i) Prince sends reinforcements to Salisbury. ii) Warwick re-joining the Black Prince.

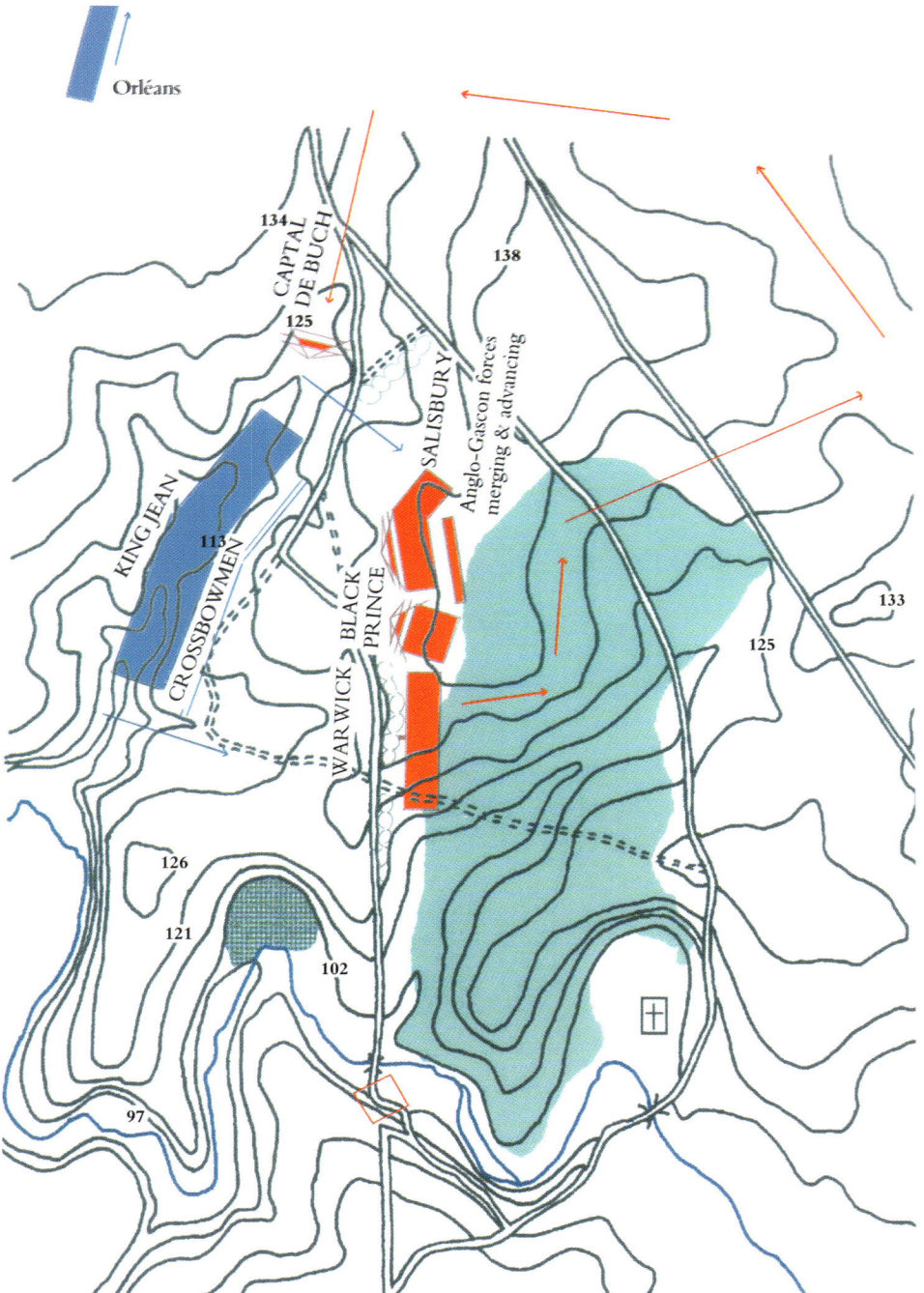

Orléans

134 CAPTAL DE BUCH

125

138

SALISBURY

Anglo-Gascon forces merging & advancing

KING JEAN

113

CROSSBOWMEN

BLACK PRINCE

WARWICK

133

125

126

121

102

97

5. The Final Clash. French: King Jean preceeded by crossbow screen. Orléans retiring. English: Captal's flank attack. Black Prince and Salisbury advance. Assumption that much of hedge screen beaten down. Diagrammatic: Jean's force shown enhanced by some of: a) Dauphin's survivors; b) part of Orléans squadrons.

Overleaf 6. Mounted men-at-arms showing a version of the barrel-style helm and visored and open bascinet.

7. Arms of Edward III, Westminster Abbey – W. St John Hope, *The Stall Plates of the Knights of the Garter*, 1901. The quartering of the French and English arms was a graphic assertion of Edward's claim for the throne of France.

Opposite above 8. *Chevauchée* – although many of the expeditionary forces on the 1355 and 1356 raids were mounted, several marched on foot including the 300 archers recruited by the terms of the prince's indenture. Troops are depicted wearing a variety of helmets and chapels de fer.

Below 9. The success of the Anglo-Gascon army at Poitiers was due to the combination of archers and infantry, both light troops and dismounted men-at-arms. Contemporary illustrations emphasised the claustrophobic conditions of battle and, while often graphic in their depictions of slaughter, were bright and decorative works. Such images complemented the manner in which a number of chivalric authors such as Froissart and Chandos Herald described warfare.

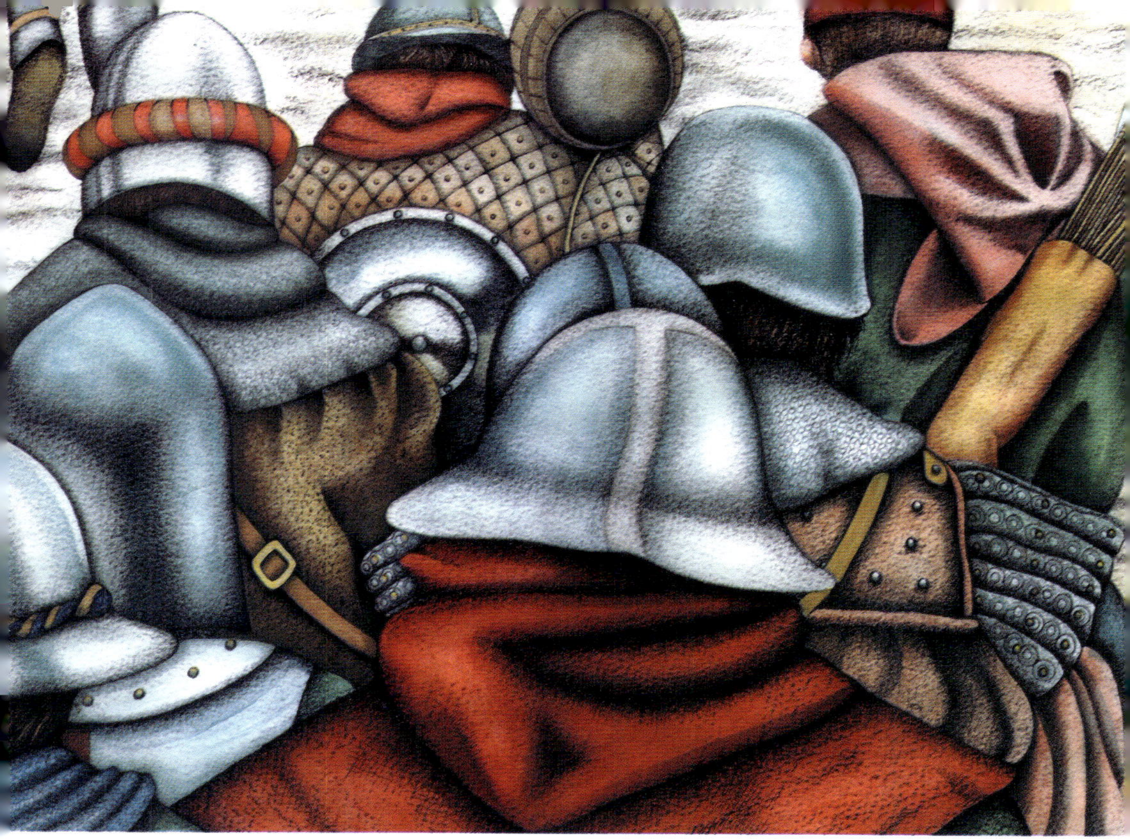

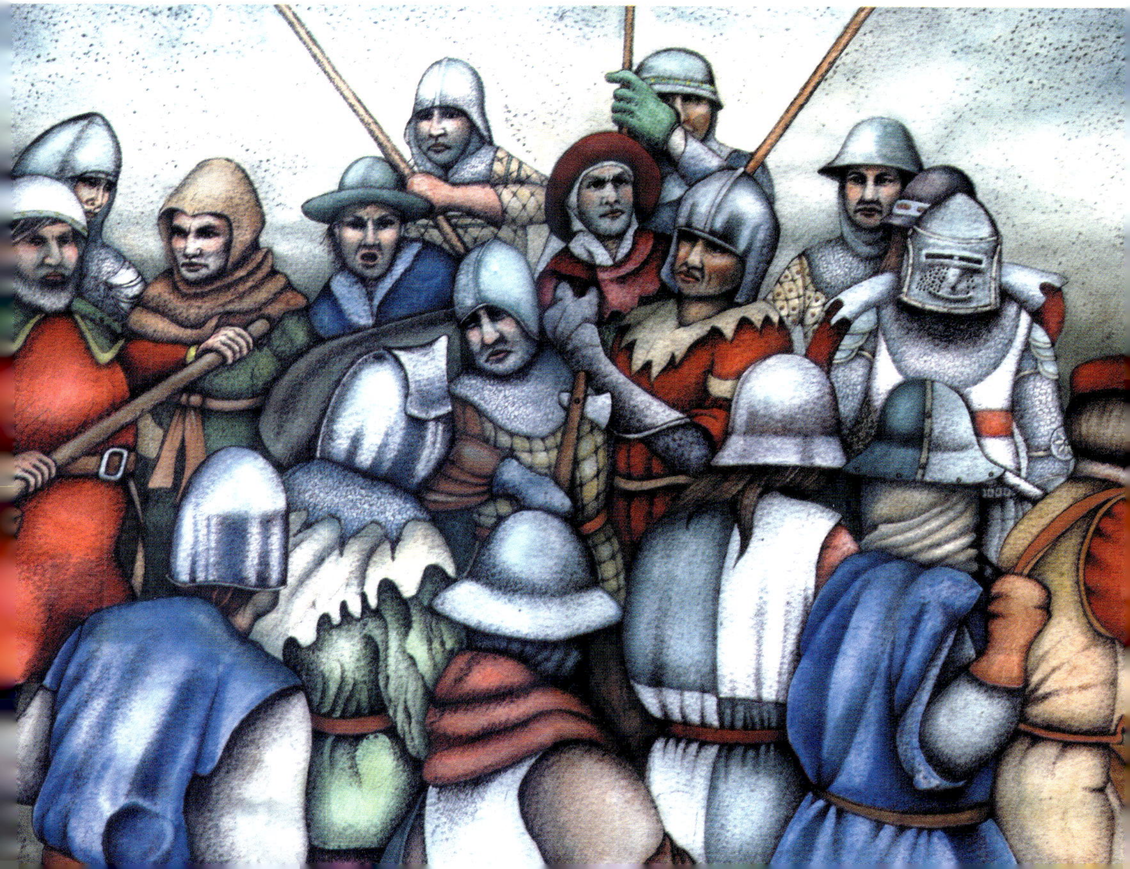

10. Stall plate of Sir John Chandos, Order of the Garter, St George's chapel, Windsor – W. St John Hope, *The Stall Plates of the Knights of the Garter*, 1901. A founder member of the Order of the Garter and one of the most celebrated chivalric figures of the age, Chandos died at Lussac while fighting in defence of the principality of Aquitaine in 1370.

11. The Anglo-Welsh longbowmen at Poitiers disrupted the French attack at a distance, killing many. At close range a clothyard arrow could penetrate plate armour. The defeat at Crécy in which the unprotected French horses had been targeted by the English archers led to a change of tactics in 1356 so that the bulk of the French army fought on foot.

Overleaf 12. The Black Prince kissing the standard of St George after the battle. Note the surcoat bearing the arms of France and England.

Pages 14 & 15. 13. The use of cavalry became increasingly outmoded in the course of the fourteenth century. However, the charge with lance and subsequent use of swords could be particularly effective. At Poitiers, the course of the battle was swung decisively in the Black Prince's favour when the captal de Buch led a cavalry attack on the rear and flank of King Jean's army.

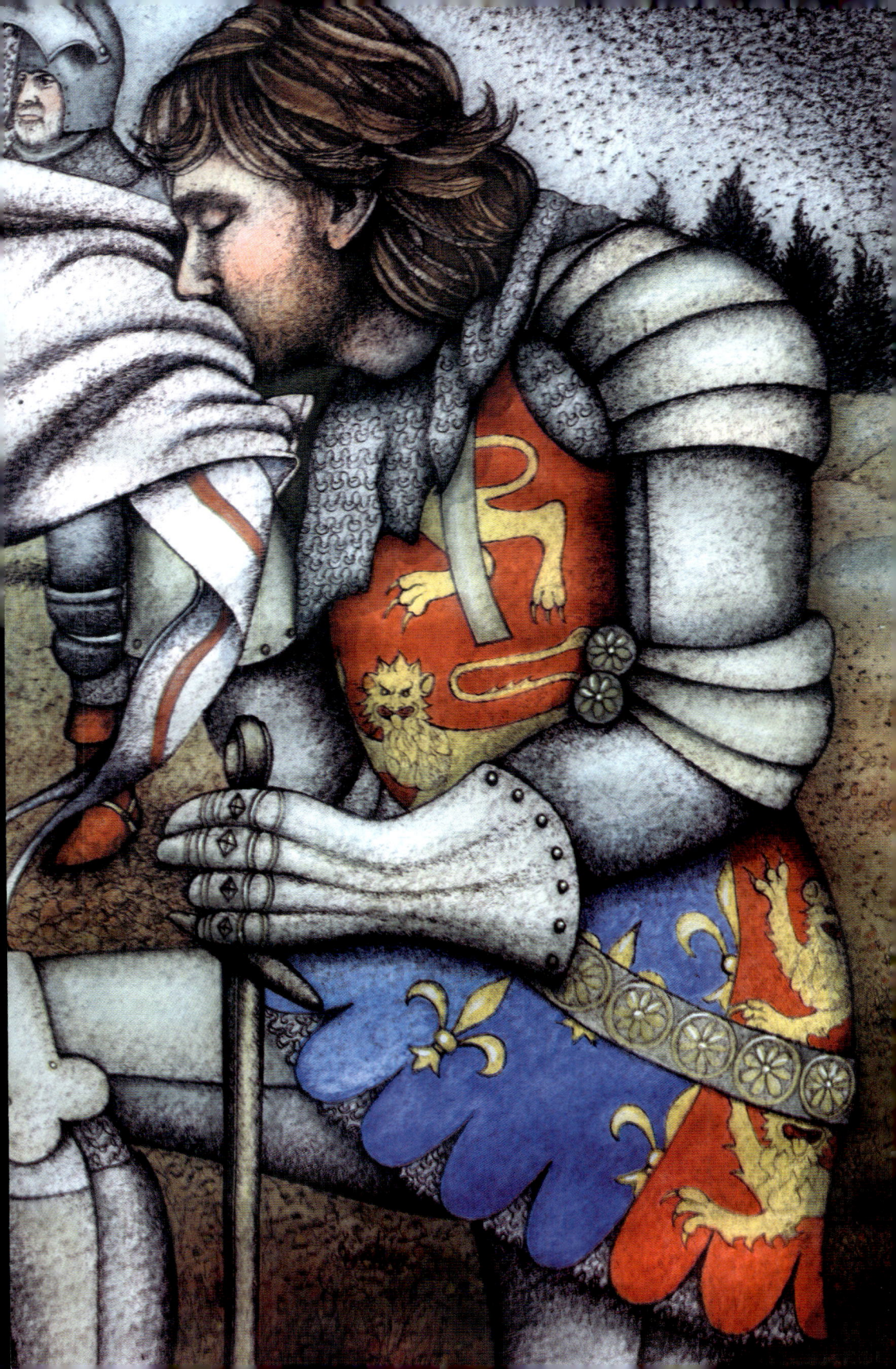

14. Stall plate of Sir John de Grailly, captal de Buch, Order of the Garter, St George's chapel, Windsor – W. St John Hope, *The Stall Plates of the Knights of the Garter*, 1901. A key Gascon supporter of the English, his appeal for support led to the 1355 campaign. He led the encircling cavalry assault at Poitiers which swung the battle in the prince's favour. He died in the captivity of Charles V after refusing to forswear his allegiance to Edward III.

12. The Anglo-Welsh longbowmen at Poitiers disrupted the French attack at a distance, killing many.

13. Tomb of Sir Nicholas Dagworth (d. 1402), Blickling church, Norfolk. The son of Sir Thomas and heir to estates in East Anglia, he forged a military career through service with the Black Prince at Poitiers and later as captain of Flavigny in Burgundy. He fought in the Castilian campaign of 1367 and after the reopening of the Hundred Years War he became closely linked to the English royal household receiving an annuity of 100 marks and became a knight of Richard II's chamber.

that they caused, to be a most effective military asset. The manner in which they were used and disposed on the battlefield, however, is also somewhat opaque.

The formation and disposition of the archer corps was described by Froissart, 'a la maniere d'une herce' which, according to Oman and Burne, was a triangular formation with the apex facing the enemy placed between divisions of dismounted men-at-arms. This is based on the translation of *herce* as 'harrow'. Alternatively, they may have been placed on the flanks or in the shape of a candelabrum; a horn-shaped projection on the wings of the army; or a hedgehog possibly using stakes or pikemen for protection.[14]

It appears likely that troops' dispositions were not standard but dependent on a number of contingencies. At Crécy, the archers seem to have been used on the wings in a forward flanking position. They may have begun the battle beyond the front rank of dismounted troops to allow them to gain a little extra range but it may be that they had a more mobile role, and after the enemy approached they fell back to the flanks curving slightly forward to provide crossfire. In this position, they would not have provided the vanguard with much protection. Due to the numbers involved and the lie of the land in 1346 it may be that the front was almost a mile in length. This allowed only a very light defence of the prince's division (the vanguard) which, at Crécy, fought in the centre. Formations at Poitiers are less certain but again archers seem to have been used on the wings and targeted, when possible, the less armoured flanks and rears of the French infantry and cavalry.

Whatever the formation and disposition of longbowmen and whatever the nature of the bows themselves, archers formed an integral part of the English tactical system from the 1330s, seeking to slow or disrupt an enemy advance. At Crécy, the bowmen proved very effective against the French cavalry and at Poitiers against dismounted men-at-arms at close range. These battles also showed the superiority of the longbow over the crossbow in terms of effective range and rate of fire. The success of the archers in 1346 made a profound influence on English tactical thinking, reinforcing concepts developed in Scotland, and also on the Black Prince and his retinue, many of whom first saw military service in 1346. The battle of Crécy thereby laid the foundations for the battle that was fought outside Poitiers ten years later and influenced the structure of the Anglo-Gascon army both proportionally and tactically. The importance of archers and their longbows was such that they became the subject of a number of governmental ordinances. In 1357 and 1369 the export of bows and arrows was forbidden and in 1365 archers were forbidden to leave England without royal licence. In 1363, instructions were issued requiring everyone, including the nobility, to participate in regular archery training and practice.

The use of the longbow, a popular, not aristocratic weapon, demonstrated the need of the king to draw on the support of all levels of society in his (at least theoretical) quest for the French throne. The success at Poitiers further influenced the composition of English armies in France. The Reims campaign (1359–60) witnessed the full emergence of the mounted archer and establishment of mixed retinues (men-at-arms and archers). This in turn led to a shift in the social composition of the military community as knights and mounted men-at-arms were becoming less significant in terms of the manner in which they might influence the outcome of a battle. Further, heavy cavalry was not conducive to conducting wide-scale, extensive raids. Lightly armed mounted troops gave the necessary mobility that allowed them to participate fully in *chevauchées* and for such raids to become engrained as the predominant strategy while a balanced troop composition allowed for an effective and flexible tactical response to a variety of military situations. Such forces were particularly effective when used in defensive positions, preferably prepared in advance or chosen for their advantageous terrain and natural features. The massed power of the archers could thin out the enemy at a distance and slow their advance and disciplined infantry would deal with any opposing forces which reached the front line.

However, the longbow was not all-powerful and the tide began to turn against the English in the Hundred Years War as the French continued to experiment with various tactics to negate its influence on the battlefield. It does not appeared to have had the same impact in 1356 as it did at Crécy, partly due to the French use of dismounted troops advancing slowly under cover of their shields. Charles de Blois and Bertrand du Guesclin at Auray (1364) also demonstrated that close formations of well-armoured soldiers could provide a less easy target. However, both were defeated and this was due to the disciplined fighting of the infantry who were entrenched in a well-defended position. Once du Guesclin became constable of France he employed what were essentially guerrilla tactics and refused to be brought to battle. If it could not be employed in substantial numbers against an enemy willing to take the initiative to attack then the longbow was all but useless.

5

AFTERMATH: PRISONERS AND THE TREATIES OF LONDON AND BRÉTIGNY

The Black Prince returned with his prisoner to Bordeaux and negotiations began almost immediately for his release. These negotiations formed the backdrop to Anglo-French relations over the next few years. King Jean was not, of course, the only prisoner to be taken captive at Poitiers, indeed the battle was extraordinary, by late medieval standards, for the number of prisoners taken.[1] As opposed to Crécy, permission was given for the taking of hostages, and the conditions of the battle made the capture of the great nobles in the king's division much easier. Some contemporaries complained that the French nobles had purchased their lives too cheaply and surrendered too soon but in reality there was nothing to gain by continuing the fight and everything to lose. It is also a very unlikely explanation of the French defeat. In 1352, partly in response to the establishment of the Order of the Garter, although a similar project had been in mind since 1344, Jean II founded the Company of Our Lady of the Noble House, commonly called the Company of the Star. It was a monarchical order of knighthood with a number of privileges and obligations, one of which was never to flee from battle. It is recorded that at the battle of Mauron in 1352, eighty-nine members of the company died because of their oath never to retreat. A number of the much-depleted company were also at Poitiers (as indeed were many members of the much smaller Order of the Garter) including the king's sons, Jean de Melun, Jean de Clermont, Charny and Armagnac. Charny, who was the author of a number of chivalric manuals and treatises, some probably written for the Company of the Star, died at Poitiers, and it seems unlikely that these were men who would retreat or surrender, especially in the presence of their king, unless there was no other option.[2]

It is impossible to be precise about the number of captives; chronicle accounts range in number between 1,000 and 3,000 and the most recent study suggests that a figure of about 2,000 is probable. The situation that this provided was novel, problematic and offered a range of opportunities for Edward III and the Black Prince. There was clearly a financial benefit that could accrue from ransoming some of the exalted figures taken captive and more particularly there were political benefits. However, for the majority of the 2,000, the financial gains were limited and the political opportunities virtually non-existent and most of them were released within weeks upon payment or the promise of payment to their captors. There were seventeen individuals, however, who were considered to be of national importance and after the return to Bordeaux the prince and his father purchased the rights to these prisoners from those who had taken them captive. The total cost to the royal purse was around £65,000, £20,000 of which was pledged to the Black Prince. Surprisingly, the great majority of money due to Anglo-Gascon captors from the Crown was paid. The prince himself however, received just over a third of the sum due to him but the residual amount might be said to be provided in the grants made in the establishment of the principality of Aquitaine in 1362/3.

The financial benefits to the English Crown however, are difficult to establish for many of these prisoners. Indeed, with the exception of King Jean, it is unlikely after the outlay and expense of maintaining such noble figures in England and Bordeaux that Edward was any better off financially. His motivation in purchasing them was political and he hoped to acquire some influence over them. He also managed to remove the king and a number of his leading councillors and nobles from positions of power and influence leaving France without guidance or direction and, hopefully, willing to accept a peace treaty on English terms. In the event, although it weakened his position at Poitiers, Jean's decision to dismiss Charles, the dauphin, from the field proved extremely significant. Without his steadying influence, the turmoil after the battle might have been even greater and the experience of ruling in these troubled times provided an excellent training for one of the most gifted and capable of French monarchs.

Jean was brought to England and treated as his status demanded. The journey from Bordeaux to London (11 April–24 May 1357) is vividly described by Froissart and the author of the Anonimalle Chronicle. The party was met by various magnates and the king himself and there was much pageantry and a number of displays and diversions en route. King Jean entered London on a white courser and the prince followed him on a black hackney.[3] The king was then lodged in the duke of Lancaster's palace of the Savoy.

The first concrete agreement between the sides was the First Treaty of London which was concluded on 8 May 1358. Negotiations, encouraged by the papacy, had continued after the truce had been established at Bordeaux on 23 March 1357. Jean's ransom was set at 4 million gold *écus* (£666,666). In addition, the restoration of all English lands in Aquitaine and Ponthieu, as well as Calais, was demanded. Nothing was offered in return; it was a ransom agreement, not a peace treaty, and Jean's willingness to concede was prompted by his fear for France and his own desire for freedom. However, by accepting a ransom, Edward III implied that he accepted Jean's position as king of France. The first instalment of 600,000 *écus*, which was to be paid before the release of the king, was not delivered by the agreed date of 1 November.

The second treaty, signed on 24 March 1359, was much more demanding. In return for the release of Jean and (on this occasion) Edward's renunciation of his claim to the French throne, the English king demanded nothing less than the return of the Angevin Empire with the addition of Ponthieu, Boulogne, Guînes, and Calais in full sovereignty. The French were to pay 3 million *écus* by 1 August 1359, and a further million was to follow, to be guaranteed by the taking of royal and noble hostages. The territorial demands were so great that Edward may have agreed to give up his claim to the throne, knowing that the treaty would never be accepted and that this would provide him with an excuse for a further invasion. Even if this did not give him the throne, it would put further pressure on the French to accept his terms for a territorial settlement. The truce that had been agreed at Bordeaux was extended from 9 April to 24 June 1359.

The French failure to comply with the first treaty was based less on unwillingness than on the inability to raise the necessary revenue. By 1359, the dauphin (the future Charles V) had restored control. The threat posed by the Jacquerie, the mercenary companies, and Charles 'the Bad', of Navarre, had been reduced, and the French council was in a position to resist a potential English invasion. Jean and his advisers, who were held captive in England and may have believed that the invasion force that Edward III was recruiting would destroy or capture France, did not know this. In May the French Estates General refused to implement the treaty and both sides prepared for war.

The Reims campaign of 1359–60 involved one of the largest single forces gathered by the English in the Hundred Years War. The English marched from Calais to Reims, the coronation city of France, and Edward intended to take the city, by force if necessary and there have himself crowned with the crown that he brought with him in his baggage train for that express reason. It failed. The people of Reims were not as friendly as Edward had hoped and they had had plenty of time to prepare defences and lay in stores that proved more than adequate. By contrast, the English found the siege extremely difficult. Food was difficult to find and forage for the horses almost impossible. It seems to have been this that drove the king finally to lift the siege and look elsewhere for his victory. First he rode to Burgundy and by means of a hefty financial inducement managed to secure the support of some of the local nobility. Next he rode to Paris.

The battle of Poitiers had galvanised the building of fortifications within France, indeed the English victory at Poitiers to a degree prevented a successful siege of Reims since the town's defences were greatly improved in the years between 1356 and 1359. Castles, churches and manor houses were all fortified. In many cases these were 'official' fortifications but they also provided sanctuary for those whose living was dependent on war. 'These fortifications were the centres of 'borrowed' lordships which provided for their occupants in the long intervals between the grander military adventures... The professional soldiers who occupied them were... freebooters... because they made a living out of soldiering without depending on the wages paid to them by their sovereign.'[4] Such men were to prove a great nuisance for the Valois monarchy during the early years of the 1360s.

In Paris, the dauphin, Charles, later to be Charles V, was a very different man from his father and grandfather. He was not drawn out as Philip had been in 1346 or Jean ten years later. He waited and watched as the English battered themselves against the walls in one of the bleakest winters in memory. Finally on what became known at Black Monday, 13 April, a truce was agreed at Brétigny.

The treaty of Brétigny of 8 May 1360 marked the end of what we might call the first period of the Hundred Years War. Formal hostilities were brought to a conclusion through a settlement involving the transfer of a captured king and the renunciation of the English claim for the French throne in return for nearly a third of the kingdom of France and a sizeable cash incentive... at least in theory. More properly the treaty of Brétigny should be known as the treaty of Brétigny-Calais for it was at the coastal town that the final clauses of the settlement were to be signed and the agreement completed. For some reason or reasons, they weren't.

At Brétigny, Edward III agreed to give up his French title. At Calais, on 24 October 1360, this was delayed. The agreement stipulated that Aquitaine, Poitou, Ponthieu, Guînes, Calais and its march were to be handed over to the English with full sovereignty and Jean would be returned for the kingly sum of 3 million *écus*. Edward would renounce his claim to the French throne as well as Normandy, Anjou and Maine. These were essentially the same conditions as in the first treaty of London although the ransom was somewhat reduced. However, by the time of the signing of the treaty at Calais, not all the promised territories were in Edward's hands. In order to guarantee their handing over it appears that Edward had the clauses concerning the renunciations of claims removed from the main document and placed in a separate document which envisaged that the transfer of lands would happen by 1 November 1361 at the latest. The renunciations would then be made orally and ratified in writing by 30 November. In the interim, the king of France would refrain from exercising his sovereignty in the territories in question and Edward would drop his French title. The mutual renunciations were never performed.[5]

Whether this was deliberate on one side or the other to provide a loophole for the resumption of hostilities is unclear, although it does seem unlikely. In a sense the capture of King Jean at Poitiers created as much of a problem as it provided an opportunity. After Edward had failed to capture Reims, Jean was only useful as a ransom prisoner – if he was to be ransomed as a king, then Edward had to accept his kingship. From 24 October 1360, Edward III refrained from using the French title, although, perhaps significantly he continued to use the *fleur de lys* as part of his coat of arms. It appears that both Jean and Edward saw the treaty as tenable and that they thought it marked both an end to England's claim to the throne and of French sovereignty in England's continental possessions.

If Edward III truly believed he could have become king of France then the treaty of 1360 was a failure. If he had fought the war primarily to secure full sovereignty over his continental possessions then it was a triumph. Different interpretations continue and abound. In many ways, it seems to me, that students of the period have been somewhat dogmatic in their interpretation of the war in general and particularly the treaty of Brétigny-Calais. Motivations change, opportunities develop, conditions evolve. There does not seem to have been enough acceptance of such a basic interpretation. For Edward, the throne of France and his claim to it may have been nothing more than a simple bargaining chip in 1337. After Crécy, after Poitiers, after the depredations to France caused by the English *chevauchée* policy and by the Black Death, by the revolt of the Jacquerie and turmoil in Paris caused by Etienne Marcel, by the financial implications of the king's ransom and the need for town and coastal defences, after all these things, the throne may have seemed something more attainable.

Conclusion

Poitiers, the Black Prince and his Military Retinue

The battle of Poitiers confirmed the military reputation of the English and more specifically of the Black Prince and those who rode with him. It was a national reputation that had risen from the nadir of Bannockburn so that after 1356, the English were known as being among the finest soldiers in Christendom. The victory at Poitiers was dependent, in many ways, on another triumph for the English in France ten years earlier although the similarities between the encounters are limited except in terms of broad strategy and personnel and, to a degree, luck. As Froissart commented '...at the battle of Poitiers, fortune was very mean and cruel for the French, and quite similar to that of Crécy'.[1]

Although the prince played a very limited role in the strategic and tactical decision-making in 1346, Edward III attributed the victory to his son. The expedition proved to be the foundation upon which the Black Prince built his career and it shaped the ideals and expectations of a nation. In more prosaic and practical terms it also reinforced specifically military ideas. The campaign was not the first to put into practice the developments that have been described as the Edwardian military revolution but it established the *chevauchée* as the predominant means of waging war in France and proved the advantage of mixed retinues of men-at-arms, infantry and archers fighting in a defensive formation and situation.

The concept of a military revolution has been much debated and Michael Robert's original thesis has been extended chronologically by some to include the period of the Hundred Years War. There are some areas of the thesis which certainly bear upon the changes being instituted in England and later in France. The war itself encouraged change both on the battlefield and the means by which troops were supplied, armed and recruited. This gathered further momentum with the development of effective artillery in the fifteenth century. The campaigns of Henry V showed the implications of artillery for siege warfare and the ordinances of Charles VII capitalised on such developments and allied them to the potential power of the emerging nation-state. By the end of the war, France had a fully professional army and emerged from 116 years of devastation while England slunk into her own civil war.

This would have seemed inconceivable to the English victors in 1346. The military experiences of the prince in the victory at Crécy and the subsequent capture of Calais were highly significant. Many of his future retinue were involved in the campaign, the most illustrious of whom were to be numbered among the Order of the Garter. 'The scale and importance of that mighty victory encouraged a bond between those who had fought there...'[2] The Crécy campaign 'blooded' the prince and his retinue and provided its foundations in terms of personnel and the application of strategy and tactics. These were to be implemented when the prince took his first independent command.

By 1355, the prince's retinue was a close-knit organisation beginning to develop into an affinity worthy of the heir-apparent. It was a group that was broadly associated with Edward III's foreign struggle and linked particularly through the role played by the Black Prince. This is evident in a number of ways, links between members of the retinue can be seen in a variety of domestic, administrative and political activities. Perhaps more

14. Memorial brass of Sir Hugh Hastings, d. 1347, Elsing, Norfolk. One of the finest and most elaborate brasses in England and one of the last in an East Anglian tradition that was ended with the onset of the Black Death. Hastings was closely involved in the military operation of 1346, leading a diversionary raid from Flanders. His brass (this is a reconstruction) also bears the images of a number of his most illustrious comrades in arms.

telling are those statements which were left for posterity. Around the sides of the tomb of Reginald 1st Lord Cobham (d. 1361) at Lingfield is a series of coats of arms showing the families of Berkeley, Stafford, Badlesmere, Ros, Paveley, Mortimer, Bohun, Vere, Arundel, Cosington and Burghersh, all of whom fought with the Black Prince and most of whom participated in the 1355–56 expeditions. It indicates 'the sense of companionship and pride felt by Edward III's military élite.'[3] Such fraternal feeling is also evident in the Gloucester cathedral window dedicated to the fallen at Crécy and the memorial brass of Sir Hugh Hastings at Elsing in Norfolk. In later years Sir Thomas Erpingham, who commanded the archers at Agincourt, dedicated a window in a Norwich church to all those knights of Norfolk and Suffolk who had fought in the wars with France and died without a male heir. A number of the Black Prince's retinue were among them. They also were remembered as part of the military élite.

The most powerful national statement of the shared military struggle was the Order of the Garter itself. Founded in celebration of the triumph at Crécy, the Garter bound together as a brotherhood its members who were representative of the shifting international coalition shaped by Edward III and his successors against France.

The military experience at the prince's disposal in 1355 was very considerable, and together Edward and his commanders implemented the military policy which they had witnessed to such good effect in Normandy. The 1355 *chevauchée* proved to be a classic example of a strategy used throughout the war to great psychological and financial effect though, in that instance, it failed to recoup great territorial or political gains. By contrast, the raid of the following year culminated in the battle of Poitiers. '...there died [that day]... the full flower of French chivalry'[4] and those that did not fall were taken captive alongside their king. Matteo Villani described it as 'the incredible victory'[5] and it outstripped that of ten years before and was later only equalled by Agincourt.

It may be asked why King Jean forced the issue. Why, after all he knew of the English military successes, did he engage in battle? The main reason was, as it had been in 1346, political.

Geoffrey d'Harcourt was campaigning against him in Normandy, Robert le Coq was conspiring against Valois authority, and Etienne Marcel was gathering strength in Paris. The contributions to the army had been very great and he had nothing to show for them.[6] Jean needed a victory, and with rather more luck, rather more co-ordination within the ranks of the French hierarchy and a rather bolder approach, he might have had one.

What then were the consequences of the battle of Poitiers? Essentially, the treaty of Brétigny–Calais was the conclusion of the negotiations which began once King Jean was first brought as a prisoner to Bordeaux. That agreement was to have long-term consequences of its own. If the Hundred Years War until 1360 was about Gascony and the treaty of Paris (1259), then the war from 1369 until 1420 (the treaty of Troyes) was about the treaty of Brétigny. When Richard II married Isabella in 1396, the truce that accompanied the marriage was sweetened with a dowry of over £130,000. This was offered in some compensation for the fact that the English never received full payment for Jean's ransom agreed in 1360. When Henry V led his troops to Agincourt, it was in support of his claim that the stipulations of Brétigny be fulfilled. In many ways, the victory at Poitiers shaped the Hundred Years War for more than sixty of its 116 years.[7]

Appendix 1

Wargaming the battle of Poitiers
Written with Martin Tweedy Smith

There are many problems with the precise reconstruction of the battle of Poitiers and those wishing to replay the encounter should come to their own conclusions in several cases as to the number and types of troops involved and the manner in which they were armed and armoured.

Uniforms on both sides were rare with the notable exception of the green and white checks worn by troops from Cheshire. However, the soldiers may have carried some indication of their recruiting captain, possibly following heraldic colouring, e.g. Arundel's troops wearing red and white. During Edward I's Welsh wars, English troops wore an armband bearing the cross of St George.

The available sources are much more exact about the contingent the Black Prince was authorised to recruit in 1355, although it is not certain if this precise number embarked for the duchy. It is likely that the majority of those that made the initial journey fought at Poitiers.

BLACK PRINCE'S 1355 RETINUE
ACCORDING TO INDENTURE MADE WITH EDWARD III

433 men-at-arms
400 mounted archers
300 foot archers
= 1,133 total

This included troops from:

Cheshire	300 (Leaders: John Hide, Robert Legh [Macclesfield], Robert Brown [Eddisbury], Hamon Mascy, Hugh Golbourne [Wirral & Broxtowe], John Griffyn [Nantwich])
Flintshire	100
North Wales	140 (Leader: Gronou ap Griffith)

This was augmented by troops led by the earls of Oxford, Salisbury, Suffolk and Warwick, Reginald Cobham and Sir John Lisle (d. 1355) who were the chief recruiting captains.

Total:

1,000+ men-at-arms
1,000+ mounted archers
400 foot archers
*c.*170 Welsh troops
The *chevauchée* also included sizeable contingents from Gascony.

During the break in campaigning during the winter/spring of 1355–56, Richard Stafford returned to England in search of reinforcements, particularly archers as well as supplies.

1356 Anglo-Gascon reinforcements:

600 archers (300+ from Cheshire)

1356 Anglo-Gascon re-supplying:

1,000 bows

2,000 sheaves of arrows

} probably not acquired, forced to requi-
sition all available stocks in Cheshire
and ensure continuous production

30 baggage horses + others

30 grooms

Assorted victuals – wheat, oats, fish, salt pork

THE BATTLE

Terrain

See battle plans.

Initial distance between forces should be 500+ metres

Figure Size/Scale

25 mm figures – 50:1

10/15 mm figures – 25:1

Summary Tables

It may be useful for the purposes of replaying the battle or reworking the battle under differing conditions to construct tables of combatants by troop type to the nearest 50 or 100. Players may wish to distinguish between men-at-arms, esquires, knights banneret, knights bachelor, etc. and to attribute élite or veteran status to the remaining men-at-arms and archers. Such decisions will influence the 'skill levels' of each figure/troop grouping.

The following categories may be useful:

Section:	vanguard, rearguard, centre/1st, 2nd, 3rd division, etc.
Troop Type:	men-at-arms, archers, crossbowmen, light infantry, etc.

Troop Class: élite, regular, militia/levy
Weapons: sword, longbow, crossbow, halberd, lance, etc.
Armour: light, heavy, none, shield
Infantry/Cavalry.

For example:

Section/ 'battle'	Number	Troop Type/ Name	Troop Class	Melee Weapons	Missile Weapons	Armour	Mounted
3rd division French	1	King Jean	Knight Banneret	Battle-axe	–	Heavy & Shield	No (but with access to horse)
3rd division French	2,000	Men-at-Arms (select)	Knights Bachelor	Sword	–	Heavy & Shield	No
3rd division French	500	Men-at-Arms	Veteran /élite	Sword	Crossbow	Medium & Shield	No

1356 ANGLO-GASCON ARMY

The army that rode out in 1356 was further augmented by contingents led by a number of Gascon noblemen.

Composition of Army

3,000–4,000 men-at-arms.

This total includes knights and esquires – all knights were men-at-arms but not all men-at-arms were knights – as well as 'lesser' troops. English infantry units were not uniform in size nor were the proportions of different troop types. However, the army was possibly divided into groups of twenty (led by a *vintenar*) and 100 men (led by a *centenar*), these were often put in command of foreign troops to improve communication. See below for equipment.

Captal de Buch's cavalry detachment: 60 men-at-arms, 100 mounted archers (fought on foot).

2,500–3,000 archers

Armour: leather jerkin or mail shirts, often also a helmet

Arms: longbow, sword/dagger

Longbow range: 300–400 metres. Rate of fire: 15–20 arrows per minute. The best bows were made of Spanish or home-grown yew but also elm, wych elm and ash were used. They may have had draw-weights of up to 150 lbs. The arrows were 75–90 cm in length (made of many different woods) and carried bodkin arrow-heads which could pierce plate armour at close range. Two sheaves of arrows were probably carried by each archer = 48 arrows

N.B. – mounted/horsed archers fought on foot

1,000 light troops

Armour: padded jackets/aketons and helmets

Arms: spear, sword/dagger

Commanders

Vanguard/left flank: Warwick, Oxford, captal de Buch – 1,000+ archers, 500 men-at-arms, 500 light infantry (note captal's cavalry strike in later stages)

Centre: Black Prince, Chandos, Audley, Cobham, Burghersh, Loryng, Trussel, Alan Cheyne – 2,000+ men-at-arms

Rearguard/right flank: Salisbury, Suffolk – 1,000+ archers, 500+ men-at-arms, 500 light infantry.

The disposition of the Anglo-Gascon army within these three main divisions is uncertain; the numbers given above may act as a guide but should not be regarded as more than hypothetical. It is probable that the archers were divided between the vanguard and rearguard and that the prince's 'battle' was composed solely of dismounted knights and men-at-arms.

*Other notable Anglo-Gascon knights and members
of the prince's retinue and household*

Ralph Basset of Drayton, Alan Cheyne, Stephen Cosington, Thomas Felton, Edward le Despenser, Elie de Pommiers, Maurice Berkeley, Richard Stafford, John Wingfield, Baldwin Botetourt, Roger Cotesford, Dietrich Dale, Henry Aldrington, William Bakton, Robert Egremont, Geoffrey Hamelyn, John Henxteworth, Henry Berkhamsted, John Pailington, Thomas Hampton (standard-bearer).

FRENCH ARMY

Composition of Army

8,000 men-at-arms (including knights and esquires)
See below for equipment

2,000 crossbowmen

Armour:	ridged 'kettle' hat, mail hauberk or brigandine and coif, possibly plate greaves
Shield:	pavise – large shield with a prop so could be erected in front of the soldier during the reloading procedure
Crossbow:	range: 200–300 metres. Rate of fire: five quarrels per minute

5,000–6,000 light infantry troops
Most were poorly trained (3,000–4,000 militia) mainly recruited using the 'feudal' *ban* and *arrière-ban*.

Armour:	padded leather jerkin; simple iron helmet/war hat/'kettle' hat; chain-mail collar
Arms:	halberd, sword/dagger

Those better armed (2,000), including some of the men-at-arms, were equipped as follows:

Armour:	Lorigone (mail hauberk), bascinet, coat-of-plates, large pavise or smaller tablachos shield
Arms:	halberd or barde – a long-hafted axe with a thrusting point, sword/dagger

Commanders

1st division:	Dauphin Charles, Louis d'Anjou, Jean de Berri, William Douglas, the duke of Bourbon, the lords of Saint-Venant and Landas, and Thomas de Voudenay; Tristan de Maignelay (ducal standard-bearer) – 3,000+ men-at-arms/light infantry
2nd division:	Philippe d'Orléans – 3,000+ men-at-arms/light infantry (over half left field without engaging the English)
3rd division:	King Jean, Philippe (future duke of Burgundy), count of Dammartin, Philippe of Valois, the counts of Ponthieu, Eu, Longueville, Sancerre and Dammartin, Charny – royal standard-bearer – 5,000+ men-at-arms/light infantry (including 2,000 select men-at-arms) + 500 crossbowmen
Vanguard:	Gautier de Brienne (constable, led troops on foot), the lords of Aubigny and Ribemont and a German contingent under the leadership of the counts de Sarrebruck, Nassau and Nidau – 2,000+ men-at-arms/light infantry + 1,500 crossbowmen
Marshals:	Jean de Clermont, Arnoul d'Audrehem – 300–500 cavalry (knights and esquires, heavily armoured)

Other notable French and allied knights

Eustace de Ribbemont, standard-bearer; Sir William Douglas (rode with Audrehem, brought 200 Scottish men-at-arms); Hugues de Chatillon

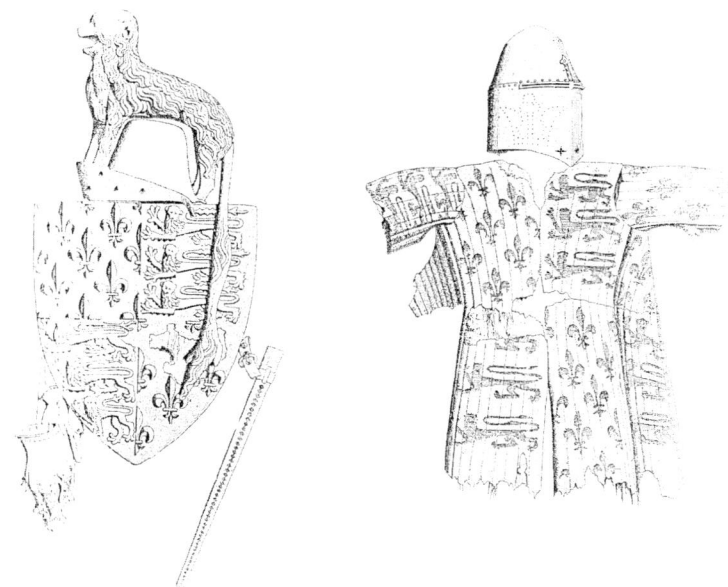

15. The funeral achievements of the Black Prince, Canterbury cathedral.

French Captives

Those wishing to recreate the battle accurately should note the period at which troops were dismissed from the field and the point at which captives were taken – see the description of the battle for further details.

Jean II; Prince Philippe; Arnoul d'Audrehem; Jacques de Bourbon, count of Ponthieu; Jean d'Artois, count of Eu; Guillaume de Melun, archbishop of Sens; Bernard, count of Ventadour; Pierre d'Aumont; count of Vendome; count of Tancarville; count of Auxerre; count of Joigny; count of Longueville; Lord Derval; Lord Daubigny; count of Nassau; count of Saarbrucken.

French casualties

Duke of Bourbon; Gautier de Brienne, constable; Renaud Chauvel, bishop of Chalons; Jean de Clermont; Renaud V de Pons.

English and French Men-at-Arms
(including knights banneret/bachelor and esquires)

The men-at-arms, comprising, in the main, the broad ranks of the aristocracy and a number of professional soldiers, were armed similarly in England and France. Apart from the small cavalry detachments led by Clermont and Audrehem, the French fought on foot in order to counter the attacks of Anglo-Welsh archers. Similarly the Anglo-Gascon force fought on foot but had access to the horses which had carried the bulk of the army from Bordeaux to Poitiers. Some of these were remounted in the later stages of the battle and led in an encircling manoeuvre by the captal de Buch and possibly James Audley.

An English or French knight did not fight alone, he was part of a small group who served his needs and protected him. Usually this took the following form –

English (described as a lance): comprising a knight, man-at-arms and two mounted archers (fought on foot)

French: man-at-arms, an esquire, three mounted archers and a hobelar (light cavalryman)

Armour: Mixture of chain-mail, *cuir-bouilli* (hardened leather) and half-plate.

Armour was undergoing a considerable evolution in this period. The wargamer may wish to arm the more experienced and affluent troops with the more 'modern' styles.

An aketon or simplified hauberk provided padding and a securing place for metal plates and areas of chain mail which protected the articulated parts and extended beyond the lower edge of the jupon. This was worn under a breast-plate which was beginning to replace the mail hauberk. This possibly had a corresponding rear plate. The plate was topped with a surcoat or jupon (more tightly fitting, shorter garment generally without sleeves, although not in the case of the Black Prince's displayed above his tomb in Canterbury cathedral).

16. Shield with royal arms from the prince's tomb.

Protection for lower limbs advanced from chain mail to *pour point* (thickly quilted fabric) through to splinted armour (full plate or white armour by the end of the fourteenth century).

Feet were covered by mail or articulated sollerets.

Helmet: two types, helm and bascinet

Helm: one piece, reinforced at the front (some with visors developing in middle years of fourteenth century), becoming more domed/pointed. Worn over a mail hood and a padded cap

Bascinet: often with exaggerated visor (pig-faced/snout-faced) with a curtain of mail (*camail*) to sides and rear

Shield: heater-shaped, becoming smaller over the course of the fourteenth century (wood covered with leather, displaying coat of arms).

Arms: Various – sword, dagger, halberd, (cut down) lance, etc. King Jean used a battle axe.

Appendix 2

Dramatis Personae[1]

Albret Family

The Albret family, members of the Gascon aristocratic élite, were intimately involved with the Black Prince's military and political career. For much of his life they acted as a bulwark against the Valois monarchy in the duchy of Gascony but in 1368 a number of key figures changed their allegiance and Arnaud-Amanieu d'Albret formed, with Jean, count of Armagnac, the main opposition and rallying point for the rebellion against Edward as prince of Aquitaine.

Amanieu d'Albret, sire de Langoiran

He was a Gascon noble who fought with the prince at Poitiers and later at the siege of Limoges (1370). He married the daughter of the sire de Langoiran.

Arnaud-Amanieu d'Albret[2]

The nephew of Jean I d'Armagnac and brother-in-law of the captal de Buch, he succeeded to his inheritance in 1358. With his

17. Coin of the Black Prince.

father, he fought for the English at Poitiers and was one of the first to pledge homage to the Black Prince when he took up the principality. He had a close, although changeable, relationship with Charles of Navarre. He sent troops against him at the battle of Cocherel (1364) but, in February 1365, he was appointed Charles' lieutenant in France. Relations with the Black Prince worsened during the preparations for the Spanish campaign when the number of troops he was contracted to bring was summarily reduced from 1,000 to 200. He led the final party over the Pyrenees and fought at Nájera in 1367. On the return from Spain he was not paid the £1,000 he had been granted after Poitiers by Edward III. The proposed *fouage* would further deplete his resources, which had been greatly damaged by the ravages of the Free Companies. In this financial context the overtures of Charles V were difficult to resist, particularly as they included the offer of an alliance with the royal family, through marriage to Marguerite de Bourbon. He was at the forefront of the revolt against the prince and, in 1372, was granted the lands of the sire de Poyanne who was captured at La Rochelle. In 1382 he became grand chamberlain of France. He died in 1401.

Bernard-Ezi d'Albret[3]

By 1355 he was a long-standing supporter of the English cause having given allegiance to Edward III in 1339 following his capture by the French and an offer of a pension from the king.

18. Coin of the Black Prince.

He fought at Poitiers and married Marthe d'Armagnac by whom he had thirteen children. One of these, Arnaud d'Albret, probably died at the siege of Romorantin in 1356.

Bertucat d'Albret

The illegitimate son of Bernard-Ezi, he led a band of *routiers* and fought at Cocherel (1364) and at Nájera (1367) with the Black Prince.[4] He was recruited by Robert Knolles for further service with the prince in 1370 and later was with Knolles in London at the time of the Peasants' Revolt (1381).

Guichard d'Angle, earl of Huntingdon, c.1323–c.80[5]

As the lord of Pleumartin, Boisgarnault and Rochefort-sur-Charente, he served the French as captain of Niort (from *c*.1346), seneschal of Saintonge (from 1350), and fought very bravely against the Black Prince at Poitiers where he was captured. However, after Brétigny he gave allegiance to England and after a short break, was returned to his office in Saintonge and later became the prince's marshal in Aquitaine (1363–71). He was joint-marshal of the army that marched into Spain in 1367, led the vanguard across the mountains, and fought at Nájera. He was involved in the defence against the French after the resumption of the war in 1369. He became a knight of the Garter in 1372 and was captured with Pembroke at La Rochelle but released in 1374. In 1376 he became governor of Richard, prince of Wales, and in the following year was granted the title of earl of Huntingdon, which had been left vacant since William Clinton's death in 1354.

Jean d'Armagnac, count of Fezensac and Rodez, 1311–73[6]

As lieutenant of the king of France in Languedoc from 1352–57, he was held partly responsible for the defeat at Poitiers. He had failed to attack the prince during the 1355 raid in which his estates had been the main focus of destruction. His ongoing feud with Gaston Fébus was instrumental in the continuing discord which undermined the prince's rule in Aquitaine. Armagnac was defeated by the count of Foix at Launac in 1362 and forced to pay a very large ransom with which the prince assisted him. He gave homage to the prince after Brétigny and fought alongside him at Nájera. On returning, however, and after having repaid the prince his ransom loan, he was instrumental in organising the appeal to Charles V, resulting from the imposition of the *fouage*, and the subsequent rebellion. He was appointed captain general of the Rouergue on 8 October 1369 by King Charles. He died in 1373 after war had again broken out between himself and the count of Foix. He married first Régine Gut, vicomtesse de Lomagne, and secondly Beatrix de Clermont.

Eustace d'Aubrechicourt[7]

Originating in Hainault, the son of Nicholas, he captained a Free Company, often in the service of England. He fought in the 1355–57 campaigns and was unfortunate enough to be captured at Poitiers, although he was held only briefly. He is said to have led an attack against a German knight called Louis de Recombes. Both were unhorsed but d'Aubrechicourt was overpowered by five German men-at-arms who tied him on a baggage-cart with their spare gear. He was later rescued and took advantage of the prisoners and plunder that were on offer. In the confusion following the battle Eustace established himself in Champagne and led raids to both sides of the Seine and the Marne. He joined the Reims campaign and raided around Autry and Manre in late December 1359. He observed the signing of the treaty at Calais in 1360 and married Isabelle of Juliers, Queen Philippa's niece. He fought with Chandos at the battle of Auray and returned at the Black Prince's summons after serving under du Guesclin in Spain and fought to restore Pedro at Nájera. He continued in English service after the resumption of the war, was at the siege of Limoges and died at Carentan in 1373.

Sir James Audley[8]

The eldest son of James Audley of Stratton-Audley, Oxford, and Eva, daughter of Sir John Clavering, he was a companion and brother-in-arms of John Chandos and one of the leading chivalric figures of his generation. In 1346, during the Crécy campaign, he fought in the Black Prince's retinue. His service there and at Calais may have ensured his membership in the Order of the Garter. In 1350 he may have fought at the naval battle of Les Espagnols-sur-Mer. In addition to military service Audley also sat on the prince's council. By 1355, when he and his brother, Peter, accompanied the prince to Gascony, he was already receiving an annuity of £80. He played a major role in the ensuing campaign and in that of the following year. His valour at Poitiers and the wounds he received there were noted by Froissart and confirmed by the prince's grant of £400 per year for life in December 1356. He was later granted 600 *écus* on the customs of Marmande. He may have fought at the siege of Rennes but was certainly involved in the Reims campaign leading a number of sorties with Chandos. He was present at Calais to witness the treaty of 1360. In 1363 he accompanied the prince to Gascony and in February 1364 was at Poitiers during an attempt to settle the question of the Breton succession. Audley did not participate in the Nájera campaign as he was appointed by the prince to remain as governor of Aquitaine. When the war resumed in 1369 Audley acted as the prince's lieutenant in Poitou and the Limousin. With the earl of Cambridge he took la Roche-sur-Yon but after its capture he retired to Fontenay-le-Comte where he died.

Arnoul d'Audrehem, b. c.1300[9]

His father was probably Beaudoin, lord of Audrehem, near Ardres and, somewhat unusually for a Frenchman, he first saw military service in Scotland in 1335 and again in support of David Bruce in 1340. In 1342 he was appointed captain of Brittany. He was part of the defence of Calais against the English siege and was captured when it fell in 1347. After his release he became captain in the Angoumois, first for the king and then for Charles 'd'Espagne' from whom he received considerable patronage.

He fought at Taillebourg (1351) and then became marshal of Beaujeu. In January 1355 he rose to the office of king's lieutenant in Artois, Picardy and in the Boulonnais. He took violent reprisals against the people of Arras when they refused to pay the salt tax.

He was a marshal of the army that met with the Black Prince outside Poitiers in 1356 where he argued with Jean de Clermont over the best plan of attack. This provoked the disorganised first assault on the English position in which Audrehem was taken captive.

He was part of the diplomatic and negotiation process leading to the failed treaties of London, and after Brétigny (1360) was delegated to raise money for the king's ransom. Somewhat peculiarly, he was granted an annuity by the English king. It cannot be said whether he won the esteem of Edward III or whether he was merely trying to buy Audrehem's support.

He became closely involved in Iberian affairs and supported Henry of Trastamara in the deposition of his half-brother, Pedro the Cruel of Castile. In this he worked with du Guesclin and negotiated with the papacy for the campaign that masqueraded as a crusade and sought to remove the Free Companies from France where they were doing a great deal of destruction during the lull in hostilities between England and France.

He fought against the Black Prince at Nájera in 1367 and was again captured and brought before a court of chivalry since he had not yet paid all his ransom from Poitiers and had sworn never to take up arms against England. Audrehem escaped punishment pleading that he was fighting against Pedro not Edward. With du Guesclin he was freed in 1368.

Charles V did not employ Audrehem again in the office of marshal but appointed him to be the keeper of the gates of Paris with a substantial pension although he continued to campaign with du Guesclin who was now constable of France.

He retired to Saumur and died soon after the beginning of 1371. He was buried in the church of the Celestines in Paris.

Ralph Lord Basset of Drayton[10]

He was born in 1334/5, the only son of Ralph Basset and Alice, daughter of Nicholas Lord Audley of Helegh. He fought at Crécy and Calais, and in 1355 gave proof of his age and did homage for his estates. He also joined the prince's army. His association with the prince during this period may have secured for him a matrimonial alliance with Joan of Brittany, the sister of the prince's brother-in-law, Jeanne de Montfort. He was involved in the skirmish at Romorantin and fought at Poitiers. On 25 December 1357 he was summoned, for the first time, to parliament. He was involved in the Reims campaign and thereafter served in Normandy. In 1361 he was granted a licence to travel to the Holy Land. In 1365–66 he joined the prince's retinue in Gascony, and perhaps was involved in the Spanish campaign. He returned to England in 1368 and was admitted to the Order of the Garter on the death of Lionel of Clarence. In 1369 he was again in France then in the service of the duke of Lancaster. He returned to England but was again fighting in France in 1372–73. Basset was again in arms in 1377–78. In December 1379 he sailed in the fleet under Sir John Arundel, which suffered greatly from the weather. In 1380 he was once more in service in France then under the command of Thomas of Woodstock with a personal retinue of 200 men-at-arms, 200 archers and eight other knights. In 1385 he served with Gaunt in his disastrous expedition to Spain. On 30 October 1386 he was a deponent at the Scrope-Grosvenor controversy. He died, leaving no children, on 10 May 1390.

Thomas Beauchamp, earl of Warwick d. 1369[11]

He was born on 14 February 1313/14 and succeeded his father, Guy, as earl of Warwick in 1315. His first military experience was

19. Warwick castle. Thomas Beauchamp was a close military associate of the Black Prince. He fought alongside him at Crécy and was constable of the army in 1355–56. He captured the archbishop of Sens at Poitiers. He died in 1369. A number of the prisoners from Poitiers were lodged in Warwick castle. The original motte and bailey fortification was begun by William the Conqueror in 1086. The lordship passed to the Beauchamp family in the thirteenth century. In the 1330s and '40s, Thomas, the 11th earl, made a number of domestic improvements. Later in the fourteenth century the east curtain wall was built, flanked by Caesar's Tower to the south and Guy's Tower (1392–93) to the north.

gained in the Scottish campaigns of the late 1330s. He participated in the Cambrésis campaign of 1339 and was at the failed siege of Tournai. In 1344 he was appointed marshal of England and it was as such that he fought in the 1346 campaign and was one of those who led the attack to cross the Somme. At Crécy he may have fought in the first division with the Black Prince. During the siege at Calais he rode and sacked Thérouanne (19 September 1346). He was among the founder knights of the Order of the Garter. In 1352 he became admiral of the fleet in the south-west. He was constable of the prince's army on the 1355–56 campaigns and at Poitiers he captured the archbishop of Sens for whom he received £8,000 in lieu of ransom from Edward III. He married Katherine, daughter of Roger Mortimer, earl of March, and their daughter, Philippa, married another of the Black Prince's military associates, Hugh, earl of Stafford. Beauchamp died of plague in Calais in 1369.

Sir Baldwin Bereford

Bereford was one of a small number of men retained by the prince for life. This grant was made on 1 October 1367, probably after Baldwin had returned with the prince from Spain. He had regularly served with the Black Prince as part of the 1355–56 expedition and he also fought on the Reims campaign. He was among the prince's household when he left to take up the principality of Aquitaine in 1363 and, in 1369, he was part of the Northampton muster role which noted that he would be accompanied by six men-at-arms and six archers. This was summoned to recruit troops for the defence of the principality of Aquitaine. After the prince's death, Bereford went on to serve Richard II. In his will, dated 4 December 1405, he requested to be buried in Chacumb priory and left bequests to a number of churches and religious institutions.

Sir Baldwin Botetourt

Botetourt was master of the prince's great horses and he was stationed at Calais by 1351. He was one of the prince's chief advisors and a member of his bodyguard at Poitiers. For his services he was rewarded with Newport manor, Essex, at a nominal rose rent as well as grants of £100 and £40 a year. In 1358 he was appointed to have the keeping of the park and warren of Buckden and Spaldwick, Hunts, and also the chase of Rising. His friendship with the prince is further marked by the gift of two pipes of wine on 1 June 1358. During the Reims campaign he attacked Cormicy with Burghersh.[12]

Gautier IV de Brienne[13]

His father had acquired the title of duke of Athens on the death of his cousin Guy de la Roche but this was lost when he died on 15 March 1311. Gautier was a refugee at the court of Naples from a very young age. He married the niece of King Robert, Marguerite d'Anjou-Tarente. From 1331 he was involved in campaigns to try and regain his inheritance but these were unsuccessful. By 1338 he had become lieutenant of King Philippe of France in Thiérache and was thus involved in the first major campaign of the Hundred Years War. He remained closely involved with Italian politics and in 1341 he was offered authority over Florence and Pisa as dictator although this did not last long and he retired to Boulogne. His second wife, Jeanne de Brienne d'Eu, was descended from an eminent family including kings of Jerusalem and emperors of Constantinople among her predecessors. He again returned to try and establish his influence in Italy but was once more unsuccessful and by 1355 was again in France where Jean II was to appoint him constable of the army on 6 May 1356. This was the office he held at Poitiers, where he died.

Sir Bartholomew Burghersh, the younger[14]

He was born into a tradition of royal service in or around 1323, the second son and heir, after the death of his elder brother Henry, of Bartholomew Lord Burghersh and Elizabeth Verdon. His uncle Henry was bishop of Lincoln and chancellor of

England. Of his early childhood little is recorded but, aged about twelve, he married Cicely the daughter and heir of Richard Weyland on 10 May 1335. They were to have one daughter, Elizabeth, who married Edward Lord le Despenser. His military career began four years later when Bartholomew accompanied his father to Flanders. He continued to serve under arms in the expedition to Brittany in 1342. In 1346 he shared in the victory at Crécy where he attended the young prince of Wales and later saw action at the siege of Calais. By this time he had also received the rank of banneret.

His service was recognised in 1348 when he was named among the founder members of the Order of the Garter. A return to military service was not long delayed and during 1349 he was involved in action in Gascony and in 1350 he fought at Winchelsea. His military links with the prince were followed by administrative appointments: in 1351 he became steward and constable of Wallingford and St Vallery and on 26 October 1353 he was appointed justice of Chester.

On 24 June 1354, Burghersh with his cousin Sir Walter Paveley obtained letters of attorney after signalling their intention to go to the Holy Land although it is most unlikely that this undertaking was fulfilled. John Gildesburgh was his squire and it was through this association that John entered the Black Prince's service.

Burghersh was a major figure in the 1355–56 campaigns during which he captured the count of Ventadour and sold him to the king for 10,000 marks. However, in the next major expedition of 1359–60, Bartholomew was among Edward III's staff, and in the course of the expedition he captured Henry Vaulx. In December, during the siege, he was involved in raiding around Cormicy, east of Reims. After the failure of that siege and the subsequent one at Paris he was party to the compromise of the treaty of Brétigny to which, on 24 October 1360, he swore observance at Calais.

In 1364, on the return of King Jean to England, he was ordered with Sir Alan Buxhull and Sir Richard Pembridge to receive him at Dover and conduct him to Eltham and the Savoy palace. On 4 April 1369 Lord Burghersh made his will at Hendine and he died the next day. He was buried at Walsingham.

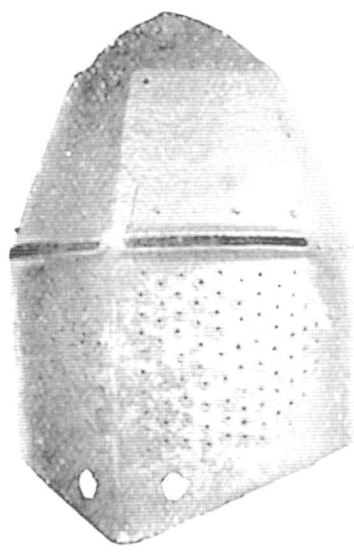

20. Jousting helm of Richard Pembridge

Sir John Chandos, d. 1370[15]

He came from a Derbyshire family and was the son of Thomas Chandos, sheriff of Herefordshire and a descendant of Robert Chandos who came over with the Conqueror. He was closely associated with the Black Prince from an early age and became his most eminent companion in arms. His early military experiences were probably on the continent and he may have been at the siege of Cambrai in 1337. However, he returned to England and fought in the Scottish campaigns and was knighted by Edward III at Boroughmuir in 1339. He was probably in the service of the king around this time and he later served as the king's chamberlain, although he was a part of the prince's entourage at times from 1337–39. In 1340 he fought at Sluys and was alongside the prince in the first division at Crécy as a consequence of which he was among the founder knights of the Order of the Garter.

He was a leading figure in the 1355 campaign. During the hiatus before the 1356 *chevauchée*, early in 1356, he was based at Brassac and involved in raiding the country around Agen. He was in command of the scouts in advance of the main army when it rode in 1356. He fought at Poitiers where he may have saved the

Black Prince's life. He was rewarded with a grant of 600 gold crowns, from the revenues of Marmande as well as an additional annuity of £40 per year.

During the Reims campaign, for which he returned to the service of Edward III and as such was described as a king's knight in December 1359, he attacked Cernay-en-Domnois, Autry and Manre with Lancaster and Gaunt. He was a party to the negotiations at Longjumeau in April 1360, which led to the treaty of Brétigny. In this year also he was created a banneret, although he would not display his banner until 1367. He became warden of Barfleur on 22 August 1360 and the king's lieutenant and captain-general in France for the transfer of lands after the treaty and later constable of Aquitaine. He became vicomte of Saint-Sauveur-le-Vicomte on 30 July 1361 and, perhaps as a result of his newly acquired interests in Normandy, on 29 October 1361 he was granted a pension by Charles of Navarre.

He also had other interests in accordance with his knightly status and had something of a reputation as a huntsman, as no less an authority than Gaston Fébus requested to see his dogs while negotiating the status of his estates with the Black Prince. One or two of Sir John's minstrels were hired by Louis d'Anjou after his death.

He became involved in the Brittany question in 1364 and on 24 February was with the prince at Poitiers seeking an agreement over the issue. He was later, possibly as a result of this, called to Brittany by Jean de Montfort. He was commander of the victorious forces at Auray in 1364 where he captured the vicomte de Fou and du Guesclin who was ransomed for 100,000 crowns. Du Guesclin remained his prisoner for some time at least until the late autumn of 1365.

He tried to prevent English involvement in du Guesclin's army which deposed Pedro but probably also argued against the wisdom of the prince's participation in Iberian affairs. In spite of his objections he led the first party over the Pyrenees. At Nájera, he and Gaunt commanded the vanguard and again he captured du Guesclin. Chandos argued that after Auray du Guesclin had sworn never to take up arms against the prince again. Bertrand argued that he fought against Pedro not Edward. The story is highly reminiscent of that concerning Audrehem and may be confused with it.[16]

He may have gone into retirement in Normandy after the return to Aquitaine or following a disagreement about the imposition of the *fouage*. However, he soon returned and was appointed captain of Montaubon and seneschal of Poitou (1369) to face the renewed French attacks. He was involved in a siege at Compeyne in June 1369 and fatally wounded in a skirmish at Lussac. He died at Chauvigny on 1 January 1370 and was buried at Mortemer. His estates fell to his sisters Elizabeth and Eleanor and his niece Isabella.

Geoffrey de Charny[17]

Charny was a younger son of Jean de Charny and Margueritte de Joinville, a daughter of the famous friend and chronicler of (Saint) Louis XI. He was probably born in the first decade of the fourteenth century and came to prominence in 1337 in his first major campaign in south-west France fighting under Raoul, count of Eu. With the opening of the Hundred Years War and Edward III's campaigns in Flanders and the north, Charny was sent to Tournai and in 1340 he was involved in the defence of the town. Later he fought in Brittany and at the battle of Morlaix where he was captured by Richard Talbot and then purchased by the earl of Northampton who soon ransomed him. He was knighted by 1343 and in 1345 joined the futile crusade of Humbert II, dauphin of Viennois to Smyrna in Anatolia. He returned in the following year but did not fight at Crécy since he was involved in the siege of Aiguillon under the command of the duke of Normandy, the future King Jean II.

Charny was closely involved in a scheme to recapture Calais by bribing the captain of the citadel, Aimery de Pavia. However, he informed Edward III, and with the Black Prince and others the town was reinforced, Charny's plan failed and he was captured once more. He was clearly considered very valuable to the new king of France, Jean, who contributed 12,000 *écus* towards his ransom. It was at this time that Jean began the formation of the Company of the Star of which Charny was a leading member and for which he was commissioned to write a series of chivalric works.

He became Captain General of the Wars of Picardy and the Frontiers of Normandy and had already been awarded the ultimate honour of bearing the Oriflamme in 1347, as he would again in 1355. It was accorded only to the 'most worthy and most adept warrior'. He was occupied in numerous diplomatic missions before his last campaign. He died fighting to the last alongside his king at the battle of Poitiers. He was buried first at Poitiers and later reinterred in 1370 in the church of the Celestines in Paris where he was laid to rest with another bearer of the Oriflamme, Marshal Audrehem.

Sir Alan Cheyne[18]

Cheyne first came to attention on 6 October 1349 when he was granted the wardship and marriage of Elizabeth, the heiress of one Thomas Praers. His career was of a somewhat mixed character and involved charges of burglary on 25 October 1352 and also patronage from the Black Prince with whom he found service as a yeoman. He married Joan, the step-daughter of William Praers, presumably related to his ward. His military skill must have been considerable as he was one of the prince's body-guards at Poitiers and by this time he may have acquired greater status in the household with the title of knight bachelor. In recognition of his Gascon service he was granted a £40 life annuity in Easter 1357.

Following the Reims campaign his annuity was increased to 100 marks and the continuing favour of the prince is evident from gifts of items of game and his appointment as constable of Beeston castle on 24 April 1363. To this was added the office of constable of Rhuddlan on 13 December 1366 for which he was paid £40 a year. He still held the post in 1385 and Richard (subsequently Richard II) confirmed his father's grants on 26 March 1377 and later once again as king. These may, at least initially, have been sinecure offices since he was probably a member of the prince's household in Aquitaine. Whether he participated in the Spanish expedition is uncertain. He was certainly summoned to the muster at Northampton in 1369 with two esquires.

Jean de Clermont[19]

The son of Raoul, lord of Thorigny, and Jeanne de Chambly, he saw service under the count of Eu in Flanders and Hainault in 1340 and then with the duke of Normandy in Avignon and Languedoc. He was rewarded on 3 November 1346 with the lordships of Boomont and Chantilly. As marshal of France (appointed in November 1352), he was sent with the duke of Bourbon to negotiate with the English and was later appointed the king's lieutenant in Poitou, Saintonge, the Angoumois and lands between the Loire and the Dordogne. At Poitiers, his argument with Audrehem led to the disruption of the opening cavalry charge and also to his death.

Sir Reginald Cobham[20]

He was the son of John Cobham and Joan Neville, and may have accompanied the young Edward III to France when he did homage for Aquitaine. On 16 April 1337, with the bishop of Lincoln, earls of Salisbury and Huntingdon, William Trussel and Nicholas la Beche, he was named an 'intimate secretary' of the king and as such was to treat with officials in Bruges, Ypres, Ghent and Flanders. At some point before 28 October 1341 he travelled to the papal curia at Avignon. He was to return in 1344 to treat with Philippe of France concerning the truce. He was also an ambassador to the French council from 18 March to 7 May 1349.

In addition to his administrative, diplomatic and political work he was an accomplished soldier. At some point before 8 August 1337 he was made a banneret and provision was made for him by the king to sustain himself in this rank. He was involved in the expedition of 1338 and in 1345 he was appointed admiral of the fleet from the Thames westwards, an office which was renewed in 1349. In c.1348 he was granted £500 a year by the king.

Cobham fought at Crécy, where he commanded the first division. He was also at Calais and Winchelsea. In 1352 he became a knight of the Garter and from at least 1353 was captain of Calais. He fought alongside the prince in 1355–56 when he was marshal of the army and was closely involved with the capture of Castelsagrat. He fought in the main 'battle' and captured the count of Longueville (his ransom was worth 6,500 florins) at Poitiers and saved King Jean from his quarrelling captors. He signed the truce of Bordeaux. He participated in the Reims expedition and died, probably of pneumatic plague, in October 1361 and was buried in Lingfield parish church. On his tomb were the arms of Cobham impaling Berkeley, which commemorated his marriage to Joan Berkeley.

Sir Stephen Cosington[21]

His early military career was in the service of Henry of Lancaster whom he accompanied in his 1345 expedition. He may have returned to England prior to or during the earlier stages of the siege of Calais. He had certainly come to the prince's attention by this time as in 1348 he gave him eight harnesses all decorated with the Cosington arms. He had a place on the prince's council by June 1351, he rode in the *chevauchée* of 1355 and fought at Poitiers where he was a member of Edward's bodyguard. As a result of this he was granted £100 a year, or lands of the same value. However, he may have been in receipt of an annuity before this. He delivered the order to Lancaster to raise the siege of Rennes as a result of the truce of Bordeaux. Following this, he spent much of 1358–59 acting as an ambassador in Normandy and elsewhere in France. Such experience may have qualified him for the commission of overseeing the transfer of land after the treaty of Brétigny. He may have been able to combine this with the duty, given him on 13 July 1360, to conduct the constable of France and other captives back home across the Channel. In this year also he was granted the castle of Saint-Sauveur-le-Vicomte, although presumably this was only for a short period as it was granted to Chandos on 30 July. He was present at the ratification of the Anglo-Castilian treaty of 1363. He stayed with Edward as prince of Aquitaine, although in April and May 1364 he was acting as an ambassador in Flanders. In addition he had close relations with Charles of Navarre by whom he was retained.

He was marshal of the army (and of Aquitaine) for the Nájera campaign and crossed Ronsevalles in the vanguard. He remained in Gascony after the return of the prince to England serving under a number of commanders in the rearguard actions. He had returned to England by 1373 when he was appointed to commissions of oyer and terminer and of the peace in Cornwall. Over the next few years he was to be closely involved with affairs in the duchy.

Sir Roger Cotesford[22]

The lord of Bletchingdon and Tusmore, Oxfordshire, he served in Scotland and was a friend of the king. As the prince's yeoman he was appointed constable of Llanbadarn castle on 23 October 1347 as a reward for his services at Crécy. As a bachelor in the prince's household he was presumably often in residence and prior to the Gascon expedition he witnessed documents alongside Edmund Wauncy and Nigel Loryng, important household officials. His friendship with the king made him an ideal conduit for news and information when the Black Prince led his first expedition and he served as a messenger between Bordeaux and London at irregular intervals between 1355 and 1358. In this role he presumably acted as a link with the king for the discussions concerning the captivity of Jean and the treaty of Bordeaux.

In 1355 he was granted the manor of Watlington for life in return for his forthcoming services in Gascony.[23] Following the victory at Poitiers, where he served in the prince's bodyguard, he was granted 40 marks a year out of the profits of Wallingford manor.

He does not appear to have joined the prince in Aquitaine in the 1360s although relations remained friendly. He became very active in county society serving on many commissions and acting as the county's MP in 1369 and 1371. He was also the keeper of Oxford castle in 1362–64, 1365 and 1368–69. He died before 20 November 1375.

Edward Lord le Despenser[24]

He was born on 24 March 1336, the son and heir of Edward le Despenser, the second son of Hugh, earl of Gloucester, and he fought in the prince's Gascon expeditions of 1355–56. With his brother, Thomas, he was frequently mentioned as being among the prince's immediate attendants in Bordeaux. He fought with Loryng and Burghersh in the skirmish at Romorantin and also at Poitiers. In 1357 he gave proof of his age, had livery of his uncle's lands (Hugh, died 1349) and in the following December he was summoned to parliament as Baron le Despenser. In 1359 he was one of Edward III's staff for the expedition to France and was among those who swore to the observation of the treaty of Brétigny at Calais. In 1361 he joined the Order of the Garter following the death of Henry of Lancaster.

In 1363 he was among those appointed to receive the king of Cyprus on his landing at Dover and conducted him to London. In 1368 he served in the retinue of Lionel, duke of Clarence, and was present at his death in Piedmont. He attended Edward III and the prince on the abortive voyage to France when they were forced to return by contrary winds. In 1373 he had command of the rear-guard of the army of Gaunt and the duke of Brittany in Picardy and Artois. He returned to England in 1374 after the truce.

He married Elizabeth, the daughter and heir of Bartholomew Lord Burghersh. Their son, Thomas, would become earl of Gloucester and a knight of the Garter. He was also noted as a friend of Froissart. He held extensive estates throughout the country particularly in Wales and the Marches. He made his will on 6 November 1375 and died five days later at Cardiff castle and was buried, according to his wishes, in Tewkesbury abbey, to which he bequeathed a chalice, given to him by the king of France.

Sir Thomas Felton, d. 1382[25]

He was the second son of Sir John Felton, lord of Litcham, Norfolk. He fought at Crécy and Calais and, as a result of his service at Poitiers, where he was part of the prince's bodyguard, he was granted £40 a year for life. He was one of the commissioners who signed the treaty of Brétigny in 1360.

He was clearly a close and trusted colleague as he witnessed the prince's marriage to Joan and such an association made him an ideal candidate for high office in the new principality. He acted as steward of the prince's household for a time after his arrival in Aquitaine before his appointment as seneschal of the principality. As such he greeted Peter of Cyprus on his visit to the principality in 1364. During the prince's Spanish campaign Felton was instrumental in gaining the support of Gaston Fébus and negotiating the treaty at Pamplona with Charles of Navarre although he did not favour involvement in Castile. After crossing the Pyrenees he led the reconnaissance party and was captured by Audrehem at Ariñez and ransomed. The ransom may have taken the form of an exchange for Audrehem who was himself captured at Nájera.

After the resumption of the war with France he was involved in action at Monsac, Duravel and Domme. He then fought with Pembroke in Poitou. Felton was also granted the sinecure office of chamberlain of Chester by the Black Prince on 20 May 1370. In 1372 he served under the command of the duke of Lancaster. On 6 March 1373(–77), after the prince had returned Aquitaine to his father, Felton was again appointed seneschal. He was again captured in November 1377 and held for three years. His freedom may have been secured by the influence of Gaston Fébus and was assisted by a grant from Richard II. He was retained by the king who, in 1381, appointed him a knight of the Garter. He did not enjoy the favour for long as he died in the same year.

He married Joan, the daughter of Richard Walkefare, for whom he managed to acquire the office of keeper of game at Castle Rising. His three daughters, Mary, Sybil and Eleanor, married Sir John Curson, Sir Thomas Morley and Sir Thomas Ufford respectively.

Sir William Felton[26]

He was a kinsman, although not the brother, of Thomas. His father was William Felton of Northumberland. He married

Jeanne de Laval, a French heiress. He fought at Crécy and Poitiers and prior to the grant of the principality of Aquitaine to Edward of Woodstock, he was appointed seneschal of Poitou and the Limousin (23 September 1361), a post he retained until his death. As seneschal he was involved in securing various castles as surety for continuing royal ransom payments.

His military skill was well known. In 1359, a case under the law of arms concerning Mathew Gournay and others was brought before him as he was considered a neutral and experienced arbiter. He was also involved in Breton affairs serving there in 1360 and witnessing the duke giving homage in Paris in 1366. In 1364 he was involved in a dispute with Bertrand du Guesclin and brought a case before the *parlement* of Paris.

He rode with the Black Prince to Spain in 1367 and was a leading figure in the large reconnaissance force to spy out the enemy. He was described by Chandos Herald as lion-hearted and caring 'not two cherries for death'.[27] By contrast Jean de Venette painted a somewhat different picture of the man, '...a valiant and noble knight, of good counsel, prudent and devout...'[28] He founded a Carmelite house at Poitiers with Chandos. He was killed in a skirmish at Ariñez, before Nájera, on 19 March 1367.

Sir Baldwin Freville[29]

There is a danger of conflating the careers of Baldwin II (15 August 1317–75) and III (1350/1–30 December 1387). Baldwin II first married Ida, the daughter of John 1st Lord Clinton of Maxstoke, and secondly Joan Dugdale. He served the Black Prince as seneschal of Saintonge. Baldwin III married first Elizabeth, daughter of John Botetourt, and secondly Joyce (her sister). He claimed the office of king's champion at the coronation of Richard II but after a protracted dispute lost the title and office to John Dymoke who had taken up the Marmion claim through marriage.

Freville may have been abroad fighting in Brittany under the command of Walter Manny when his father died on 2 October 1343. Baldwin was at least twenty-six at the time. He inherited estates throughout the country. He fought at Crécy in the retinue of William Clinton, earl of Huntingdon, and later served with Lancaster.

He fought at Poitiers and was subsequently retained for life by the prince at £40 year. In accordance with his indenture he fought for the prince in the Reims campaign. Under the prince's regime in Aquitaine he served initially as seneschal of Saintonge and the Limousin. On the death of William Felton in 1367 he became seneschal of Poitou and, in 1369, seneschal of Saintonge. He was probably involved in the Spanish expedition himself and after the resumption of the war he fought under Knolles, Chandos and Pembroke and was at La Rochelle when it surrendered. He appears to have been captured after this as William Elmham offered to pay his ransom. He died on 6 January 1387.

Sir Mathew Gournay, 1310–c.1406[30]

Despite being the son of one of the murderers of the Black Prince's grandfather, Gournay seems to have enjoyed a relatively close relationship with Edward. He served at Crécy and Poitiers before playing a leading role with the Free Companies for which he suffered imprisonment in the Tower. He witnessed the treaty of Brétigny and fought at Auray. In 1365 he accompanied du Guesclin to Spain to take the throne of Castile from Pedro. During this time he lent 11,000 florins to Enrique of Trastamara for campaign expenses in return for a promised annuity of 1,000 florins. He also befriended the king of Aragon who granted him 2,000 florins a year. His association with that country continued when in 1371 he purchased a castle there from Hugh Calveley while both were stationed in Bordeaux. He remained with the prince after the return from Nájera until 1370. In 1378 he was appointed commander of the garrison at Dax and in the following year seneschal of the Landes, an office he held until 1381 and was re-granted in 1405. In 1381 he played a major role in Cambridge's expedition to Portugal.

Jean de Grailly, captal de Buch[31]

His family were the hereditary proprietors of a fort, fourteen leagues from Bordeaux now called 'La Tête de Buch'. The lands were in the Médoc, west of Bordeaux reaching to Castillon-sur-Dordogne. The captalate had many privileges in the *parlement*, city and suburbs of Bordeaux. Jean was the son of Jean and Blanch de Foix and also the cousin of Gaston Fébus. In 1343 he inherited the title. In 1348 he was named a founder knight of the Order of the Garter possibly as a result of the vital subsidiary action in which he was involved in Gascony during the Crécy campaign. In November 1350 he married Rose d'Albret, the legitimated daughter of Bertrand. He fought with the prince in the 1355–56 campaign during which he was present at the skirmish at Romorantin and before the battle of Poitiers he led the reconnoitring party. During the battle itself he captured Jacques de Bourbon, count de la Marche and Ponthieu. As a result of his service he was, in 1356, granted the town and castle of Cognac by the Black Prince. He returned with the prince to England. Then he travelled to Prussia with Gaston Fébus. On his return from that crusade in May 1358, he and Gaston Fébus rescued the duchesses of Normandy and Orléans in Meaux during the revolt of the Jacquerie. He was a long-term servant of Charles of Navarre and in November 1359 captured Clermont in Beavoisis.

After the siege of Reims lifted in early 1360, he joined the column led by the Black Prince. In March/April he went to Charles of Navarre to try and organise a concerted effort to attack Paris. In 1360 he swore to the peace at Brétigny.

He succeeded Philippe of Navarre as lieutenant in Normandy for King Charles of Navarre after Philippe's death on 29 August 1363 and on 6 May 1364 he commanded the Navarrese forces at the battle of Cocherel in which he was defeated and captured by a Breton squire, Roland Bodin.[32] He was handed over to Charles V and later released to try and organise a peace. Charles V sought to secure his loyalty with the grant of Nemours castle. This was renounced after he was reproached by the Black Prince with whom he again served in 1367. He campaigned in Spain initially in the company of James, king of Majorca and led the final group over the Pyrenees. On 3 April 1367 he fought at Nájera in the centre alongside the prince.

In 1370 he was granted the county of Bigorre in Aquitaine by Edward III and with Sir Thomas Felton he prevented the capture of Linde. In 1371 he was appointed constable of Aquitaine, and in 1372, a governor of Gascony. In this year he was also captured near Soubise. Charles V refused to ransom him unless he swore never to bear arms against France. He declined and died in prison in 1377.

John Kentwode[33]

He was one of the prince's esquires in the 1350s and '60s. As such he fought in the 1355–57 campaign and assisted Edmund Wauncy with the capture of Philippe, the king's son, at Poitiers, for whom they were paid 4,000 marks. Continuing payments for Philippe were made partly dependent on John joining the prince in Aquitaine in September 1364, and in April 1365 his annuity was increased to 200 marks. He probably remained in Aquitaine and was perhaps at Nájera as he received letters of protection at the end of July 1366.

He was knighted by 1369 and became knight of the shire of Berkshire and as such he was one of those said to have the prince's support in the Good Parliament during which he was one of the accusers of Alice Perrers. He may also have captured the Dominican friar on whom Perrers was supposed to rely for her influence over the king. After being involved in various administrative capacities in Berkshire, he became steward of Cornwall on 26 August 1378. During Richard's reign he served on a very great number of commissions in Berkshire, Devon and Cornwall and was elected MP of all those counties. He also acted as an ambassador to Brittany and to the west country bishops, in addition to serving in a supervisory role on behalf of the king in matters regarding forces leaving for the Iberian peninsula. He also oversaw the forces of the earl of Buckingham on the Brittany expedition of 1381. This military role was to be one he was often asked to play. In July 1383 he supervised the musters of the forces serving under William Scrope and in 1386 he was involved in a similar capacity for Gaunt's expedition to Castile. After the Merciless Parliament, in May 1388, he was appointed steward of the estates of Robert Vere. Although his sympathies may well have lain with the Appellants, they replaced him with their own man, Philip Courtenay, in November 1388. However, duties were found for him elsewhere and on 25 May 1389, with others, he became a justiciar in south Wales, a post to which he was re-appointed on 17 October of the following year. He died *c.*1394, leaving a son, Reynold, who probably became the dean of St Paul's, and a widow who survived until 1404.

Sir Nigel Loryng[34]

Nigel was the son and heir of Roger Loryng of Chalgrave, Bedfordshire, and Cassandra, daughter of Reginald Perot. His career was perhaps first brought to modern attention by Arthur Conan-Doyle in his books *Sir Nigel* and *The White Company*. The earliest historical record notes the grant of a life annuity of 100 shillings issued at Berwick on Tweed in 1335 presumably as a reward for service in the Scottish campaigns. By 1 January 1338 Nigel was registered as an esquire in the earl of Salisbury's retinue but by the end of the year he was serving as a member of the king's household in the Low Countries and was described as a 'king's yeoman' and was receiving an annuity of 20 marks.

His role in the battle of Sluys on 24 June 1340, for which he was knighted, is attested by Froissart.[35] In 1342 Nigel served under Sir Walter Manny in Brittany and three years later Loryng was sent on his first diplomatic mission. With Michael Northburgh, the future bishop of London, he was sent to secure a papal dispensation for the intended marriage of the Black Prince to Margaret of Brabant. In that year he also found service with the earl of Derby and the following year was with him in Gascony.[36] While Grosmont was the king's lieutenant in Gascony he granted Loryng rights to the 'pedage' of St Macaire. He was retained for life by the prince in peace and war in 1349 and granted an annuity of £50. Prior to this he had been present at the siege of Calais with a small contingent of five men and it may have been there or through a recommendation from Grosmont that he entered the prince's service.

In 1348 he was named as one of the Garter founders and sat in the tenth stall on the prince's side.[37] He was called on for further diplomatic duties in 1350 in Flanders. The delicate situation regarding the succession and the possible role of the country in the Hundred Years War, shows that Loryng had already become marked as a skilful diplomat. It may be that he spent much of the next few years in France and particularly Gascony although it was during this period that he became the prince's chamberlain, an office he was to retain for many years.

He participated in the *chevauchée* preceding the battle of Poitiers, being part of the raiding party at Romorantin and a member of the prince's bodyguard at the battle itself. The following years, before the Reims campaign, may have been spent passing between Gascony and England on the prince's business and he may have acted as a go-between for Edward and his father, a pattern which may have been established after Poitiers when he brought news of the victory to the king. On 20 July 1358 he was granted the office of surveyor of the forest and steward of the lordship of Macclesfield. During the 1359–60 campaign he served in the prince's retinue and was involved in the negotiations preceding the treaty of Brétigny and appointed to oversee its implementation.[38] He had a seat on the prince's council in the principality. Froissart also asserts he was present at the court at the time of the visit of Peter of Cyprus.[39]

Loryng accompanied the prince on the Spanish campaign and fought at Nájera. Prior to departure he had been sent to England to discuss strategy with the king. 1369 marked his last year of known military service, first under Robert Knolles in a skirmish on the Gascon borders and later with Chandos and the earl of Pembroke. It seems likely that he returned with the prince to England in 1371 serving Edward until his death in 1376. After this he appears to have gone swiftly into near retirement.

He was the benefactor to the building of a cloister at the Black Prince's favoured abbey of St Albans. He married Margaret, the daughter and heir of Ralph Beauple. They had two daughters, Izabel who first married William Coggan and secondly Robert Lord Haryngton, and Margaret who married Thomas Peyvre.

William Montague, 2nd earl of Salisbury, 20/25 June 1328–3 June 1397[40]

The earls of Salisbury played central roles in Edward III's plans and aspirations for acquiring the French throne. Salisbury's father was a main player in the Nottingham coup which placed Edward on the throne in more than name alone and which resulted in the execution of Roger Mortimer and the forcible retirement of Queen Isabella.

He succeeded his father, although still a minor, in 1344. Two years later, aged eighteen, he was knighted alongside the Black Prince on landing at La Hogues at the start of the campaign that led to the victory at Crécy and the capture of Calais. In 1348 he was one of the first to be named a knight of the Garter after the original founders and two years later fought at Les-Espagnols-sur-Mer.

Relations with the prince were changeable and were strained over the fate of the county of Denbigh: as a marcher lord, Montague came into contact with some of the more expansionist designs of the Black Prince and his council. In 1354 he was appointed constable of the king's army in France and his military career continued in 1355 when he joined the Black Prince on campaign. At Poitiers he commanded the rearguard which routed the attack of Jean de Clermont, the constable of France. He remained abroad on service until 1360 and was one of those who negotiated the treaty of Brétigny. Following the death of Isabella, the queen mother, he inherited property and other rights. In 1363 he became hereditary steward of Chester.

After the re-opening of the war he was involved in the abortive attempt to relieve Thouars in September 1372 and was then given command of an expedition to patrol the coast which resulted in the burning of seven Spanish ships at St Malo. At the relief of the siege of Brest, Montague's challenge to du Guesclin was refused. He participated in the Bruges conference and was a commissioner to France. Montague's naval experience was briefly called upon between July and November 1376 when he acted as admiral of the western fleet. He also participated in a number of Gaunt's forays into France before receiving the captaincy of Calais in 1379. During the Peasants' Revolt he counselled the young king and accompanied him to the Tower and Smithfield. As a reward for his diplomatic service in negotiations with the king of Scotland William received the Isle of Wight and Carisbrooke castle (1382). He also held the Isle of Man but sold it in 1393 since he had no heir, supposedly he had been killed by his father in a tournament. He married Elizabeth, the daughter and subsequently the co-heir of John Mohun. He was buried at Bisham.

Sir Richard Stafford[41]

He was the brother of Ralph, first earl of Stafford, and married Matilda, daughter and co-heiress of William Camvill of Clifton, Staffs. He was the most consistent lay member of the prince's council and served from at least 1343, in which year he was one of the commissioners assigned to take control of the principality of Wales and deliver it to the Black Prince.

His service was not purely administrative, he was a bachelor in the prince's household and he probably fought in the first division at Crécy (although he may have earlier been with the earl of Derby, he certainly fought with Grosmont at some stage) and on 26 February of the following year he was appointed steward of the prince's lands. He was also involved in the Calais siege.

He fought in the Poitiers campaign where his previous Gascon experience in the service of the earl of Derby stood him in good stead as did his administrative abilities. Whilst on campaign he authorised the issue of the prince's letters. At the beginning of the *chevauchée* he was made a banneret at Bassoues on 19 October 1355. He was made responsible for the reinforcing and re-supplying of the prince's forces prior to the 1356 raid.

With Miles Stapleton and Nigel Loryng he was commissioned to investigate truce violations in France in 1360–61. From July to November 1361 in the course of the transfer of lands after Brétigny he was seneschal of Gascony and may thereafter have stayed with the prince in Aquitaine although he also undertook diplomatic duties for Edward III. However, when the prince returned from Gascony in 1371 and instigated two very major commissions of oyer and terminer in Cornwall, it was Richard Stafford who was chosen to head the investigations.

His military reputation must also have been high by this time as he, with Guy Bryan, was appointed to fulfil the duties of constable of England to hear the case of Edmund Mortimer who claimed a prisoner was being unjustly held from him by Ralph Basset. Following the prince's death he became a councillor of Richard II. He died *c.*1380.

Sir John Sully[42]

John Sully was descended from a younger branch of the Sully family of Devon. His military experience was very extensive although perhaps not quite as vast as he claimed as a deponent at the Scrope-Grosvenor enquiry. The greatest doubt lies in his participation in the early Scottish campaigns. In 1333 he may have fought at Halidon Hill and was at the capture of Berwick. On 12 July 1338 he was in France, and like a number of the prince's future retinue, serving in the company of the earl of Salisbury. His military career continued and in August 1346 he fought at Crécy where he may have come to the attention of the Black Prince. In 1350 he was involved in the battle of Les Espagnols-sur-Mer and he was retained for life in 1353 to be one of the prince's *especial retinue*.[43] Soon after, he was appointed surveyor of game in Cornwall. He replaced John Dabernon as sheriff of Devon and Cornwall but was unable to take up his office. In 1355 he accompanied the prince to Gascony and in the following year he fought at Poitiers. He was again involved in active service in 1359 when he was issued letters of protection. It may have been as a consequence of this service that in 1361 he was granted by Edward III that once each year he could hunt in the royal forests with his dog, 'Bercelette'.

His military success was noted at the highest levels and on the feast of St George in 1362 he was made a knight of the Garter, taking the ninth stall on the prince's side, in place of Reginald Cobham. In 1363 he accompanied the prince to Aquitaine and in 1367 fought at Nájera. He remained in service in France and in 1370 had further letters of protection, as he was about to serve in Aquitaine. He died *c.*1388.

Sir William Trussel

The Trussel family had served in the administration of Cheshire since the early years of the fourteenth century. William's military service with the prince commenced when he rode in the *grande chevauchée*. He received letters of protection on 9 November 1355 and continued to serve throughout the winter lull and at Poitiers where, as a bachelor of the prince's household, he was one of Edward's bodyguards. He was rewarded with an annuity of £40 from the Chester exchequer on 16 November 1363, although it would be surprising if this was the first such grant he received from the Black Prince.

He accompanied the prince to Aquitaine in 1363 but it is not certain if he was involved in the Spanish campaign. He was certainly summoned to the 1369 muster at Northampton and therefore fought in France in the defence of the principality. He died on 12 February 1380.

Robert Ufford, earl of Suffolk, 1298–1369[44]

He was born on 9 August 1298 and was granted seisin of his father's lands on 19 May 1318 and those of his mother (Cecily, daughter and co-heir of Robert Valoinges) on 16 August 1325. He had been the second son but his brother had died, allowing Robert to inherit. In March 1324 he was abroad in the service of Edmund, earl of Kent. He was created earl of Suffolk on 16 March 1337. He fought in the first division at Crécy and at the siege of Calais. He became a knight of the garter in *c.*1349 and was the titular head of the prince's council in *c.*1355, although he had been associated with it since 1337. He accompanied the prince on the 1355 expedition and fought in the Reims campaign. He died on 4 November 1369.

John Vere, 7th earl of Oxford, 1312–60[45]

He had livery of his lands in 1331 and in the following year set out on a pilgrimage to Compostela. Matters closer to home were at the forefront in 1333 when he was a witness to Edward III's treaty at Berwick. He was again in service in Scotland in 1335. The opening of the Hundred Years War saw him fighting abroad. In 1340 he was in Flanders and in 1342 in Brittany. The latter year also saw his participation in the Dunstable tournament. John returned to Brittany in 1345 with the earl of Northampton and they secured a victory over the forces of Charles de Blois. He sailed again in 1346 to take part in the Normandy campaign, and at Crécy he fought in the first division. He was again in arms with the Black Prince in 1355–56. He was one of Edward's chief advisors at Poitiers and he remained in Bordeaux while negotiations began for the ransom of the king of France.

Vere died at the siege of Reims in 1360 and was buried at Colne priory.

Roger de la Warre, 1326–70

The son of John and Margaret (Holand), he was born on 30 November 1326. He first saw military service in 1346 when he was knighted with the prince at La Hogues and fought in his division at Crécy. He was also involved in the Calais siege and received his inheritance in 1349. He was again in military service in 1355 and in the raid of the following year he was involved in the skirmish at Romorantin and later fought at Poitiers where he claimed to capture Jean.[46]

Along with a number of the prince's close military associates, his involvement in the Reims campaign was in the king's division. During this he was captured in 1360 but soon ransomed. He was first summoned to parliament in 1362 but spent much of the following years in Aquitaine. He was first mentioned on the list of those noted as part of the prince's household on travelling to Bordeaux in 1363. He may not have remained in the principality continually but certainly spent much of the time out of the principality with Edward in France. He was a knight of the prince's household and a councillor in Aquitaine.

According to Chandos Herald, he fought in the Spanish campaign in 1367. After the resumption of the war he fought

21. Tomb of Sir John Wingfield, Wingfield, Suffolk. Wingfield served the Black Prince (as did his first cousin, William). He was a key figure in the preparation for the 1355–56 expedition as governor of the prince's business and examined closely the fiscal implications of the *chevauchée* on Valois finances. He died in 1360.

under Gaunt's command in Picardy and Caux from July to November 1369. He died in Gascony on 27 August 1370.

Sir John Wingfield

He first came to prominence in the service of the earl of Surrey and then William Montague, earl of Salisbury, with whom he served at Crécy and Calais. By 1351 he transferred to the employ of the prince of Wales and became a bachelor of his household, steward of his lands, chief councillor and 'governor of the prince's business'.[47] As such he was responsible for the routine central

22. Tomb of Sir Michael and Lady de la Pole, Wingfield, Suffolk. Michael de la Pole, c.1330–89, fought with the Black Prince in the Reims campaign and during the rearguard action defending the principality of Aquitaine. He was present at the siege of Limoges in 1370. On 6 August 1385 he was created earl of Suffolk, a remarkable rise in fortune for the descendant of a wool merchant. However, as a favourite of Richard II he became a target for the Appellants in 1387 and fled to Paris. He was buried alongside his wife, Katherine, the daughter of John Wingfield, the Black Prince's business manager.

administration of the prince's estates and with other councillors was the decider of policy and controlled the activities of the privy seal. He held these offices until his death in 1361.

In the 1355–56 campaigns he was responsible for administration. During the preparation for the Reims campaign he was a central figure in acquiring revenue for the operation, and borrowed 20,000 marks on behalf of the prince. Despite this administrative role he appears to have fought in all of the prince's campaigns in the 1350s. He was sent to consult with the king over the implementation of the treaty of Brétigny. His daughter and heir, Katherine, married Michael de la Pole, the future earl of Suffolk.

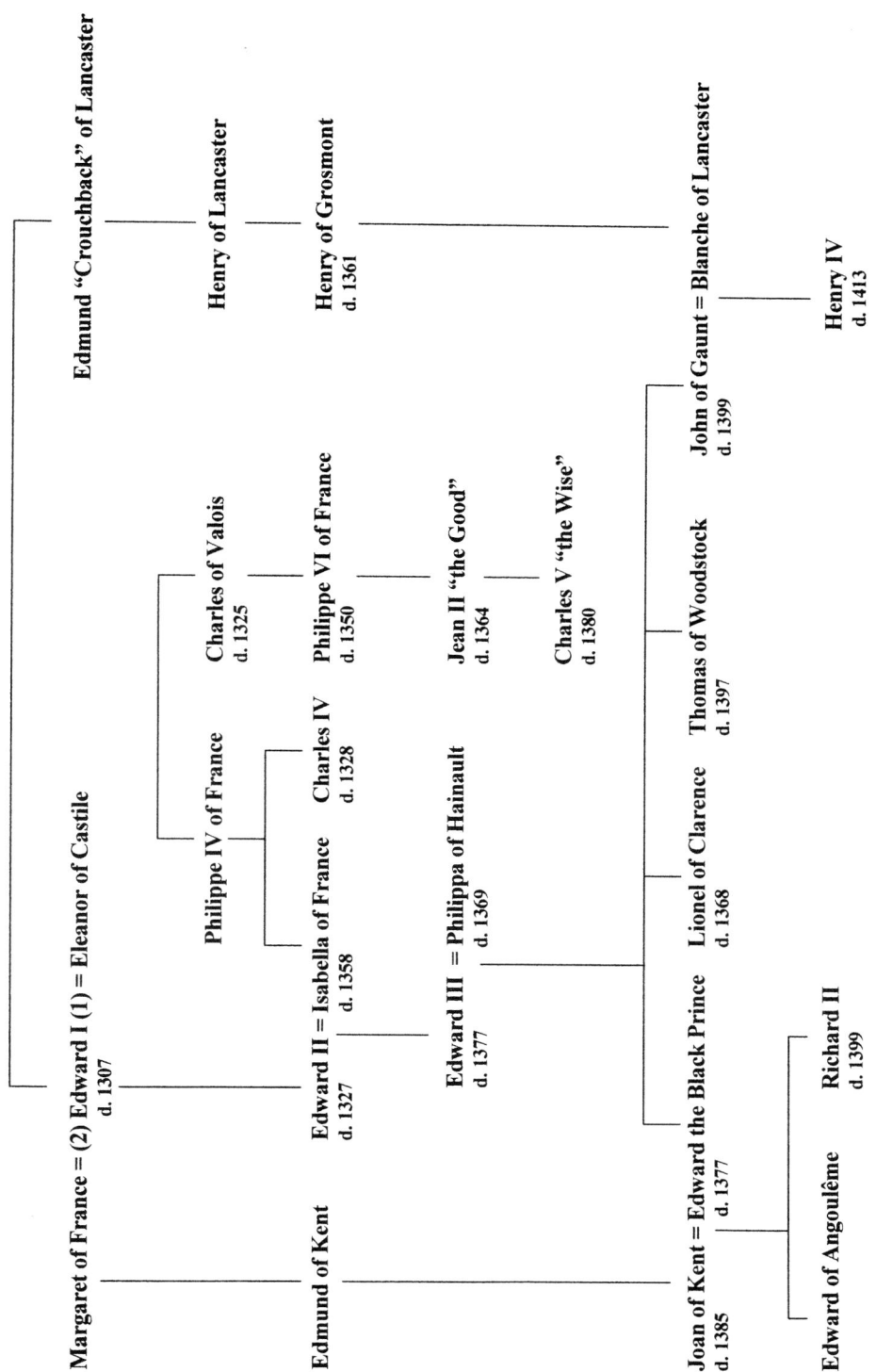

Plantagenet/Valois Genealogy.

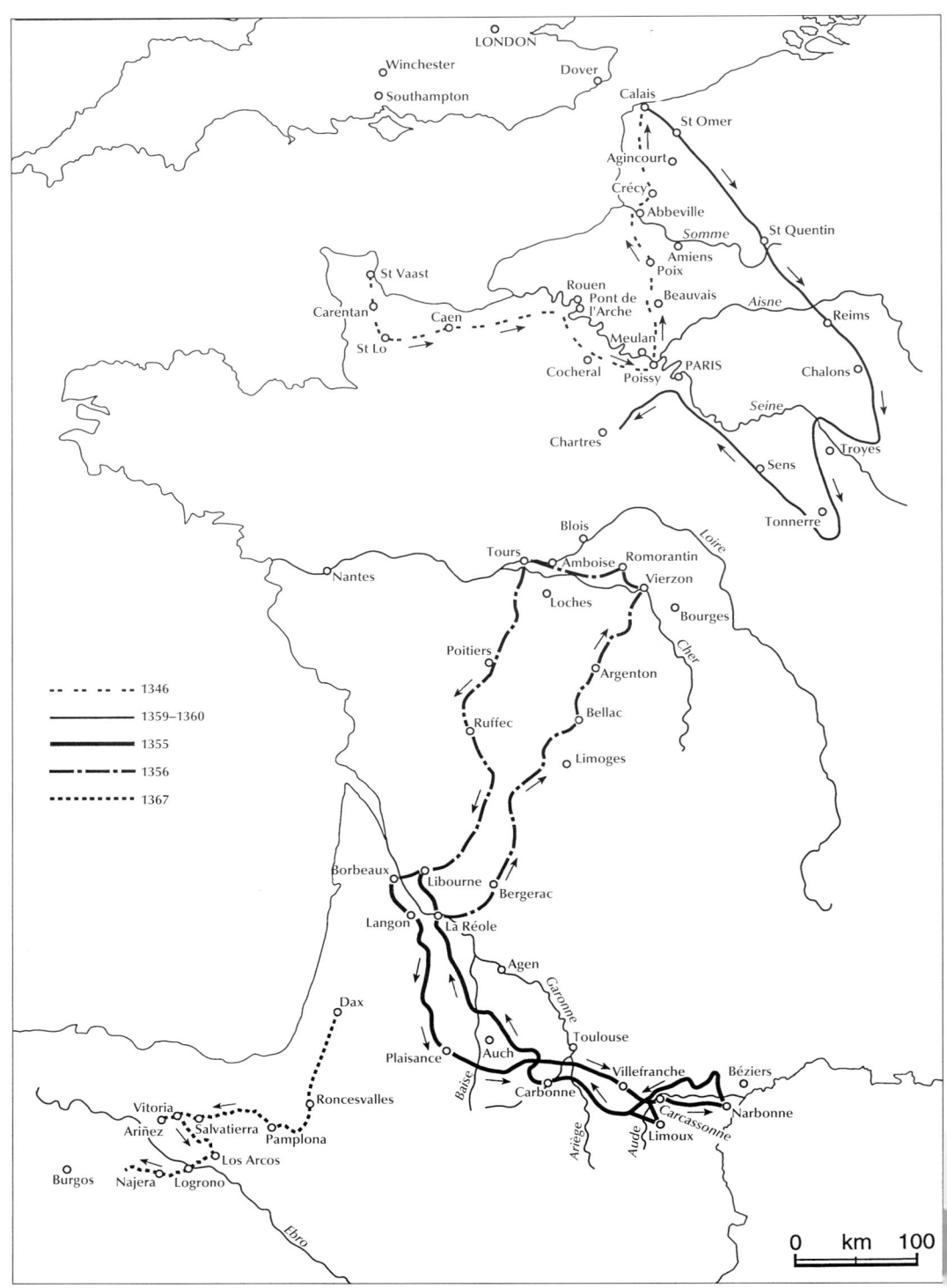

Map 1 – The Black Prince's military campaigns.

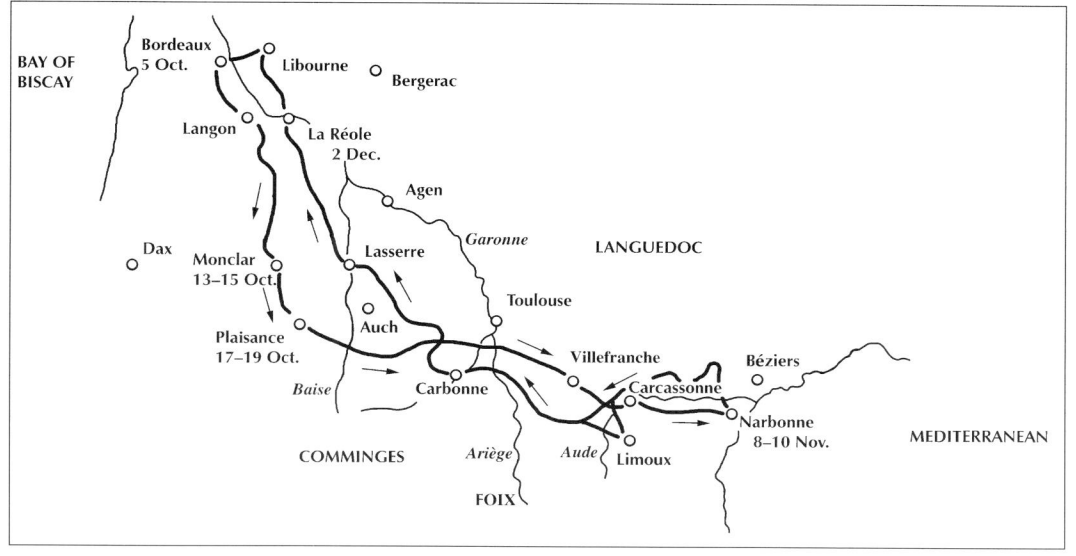

Map 2 – The *grande chevauchée*, 1355.

Map 3 – The raid of 1356.

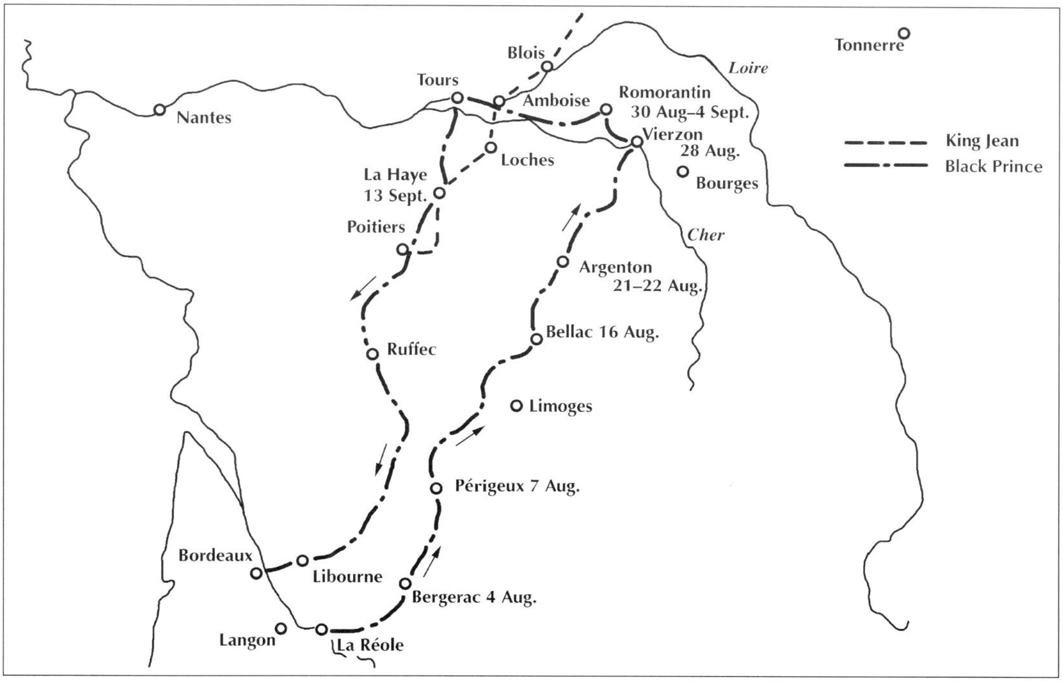

FURTHER READING

PRIMARY SOURCES
CHRONICLES AND CONTEMPORARY TEXTS

For a description of the route of the 1356 *chevauchée* from Bergerac see the *Eulogium Historiarum,* iii, ed. F.S. Haydon (London, 1863).

On the battle of Poitiers itself see *The Anonimalle Chronicle*, ed. V.H. Galbraith (Manchester, 1927), which contains unique details of the encounter.

Geoffrey Le Baker, *Chronicon Galfridi le Baker de Swynebroke, 1305–56*, ed. E.M. Thompson (Oxford, 1889) also provides a full account and includes an exhortation made by the prince to his men before the battle.

The verse biography of the prince's life written *c.*1380 by Chandos Herald recounts the battle and details the preliminary negotiations although it is most valuable for the Castilian campaign of 1367. Translations are available in the editions by M. Pope and E. Lodge, *Life of the Black Prince by the Herald of Sir John Chandos* (Oxford, 1910) and R. Barber, *The Life and Campaigns of the Black Prince* (Woodbridge, 1986). The most recent edition is D.B. Tyson, *Vie du Prince Noir* (Tübingen, 1975).

The Chronicles of Jean Froissart provide a key insight into the mentality of the fourteenth-century Anglo-French aristocracy. There are numerous editions:

Chroniques, ed. Simeon Luce (SHF) (Paris, 1870–present).

Oeuvres, ed. Kervyn de Lettenhove (Brussels, 1867–77).

The most recent, although heavily expurgated, translation into
English is G. Brereton, *Froissart: Chronicles*
(Harmondsworth, repr. 1978).

For a contemporary guide to chivalry probably written for the
Order of the Star see Geoffroi de Charny, *Livre de Chevalerie*,
ed. and trans. R. Kaueper and E. Kennedy (Philadelphia,
1996).

COLLECTIONS OF SOURCES IN TRANSLATION

C. Allmand, *Society at War. The Experience of England and France
During the Hundred Years War* (Edinburgh, 1973, repr.
Woodbridge, 1998).

R. Barber, *The Life and Campaigns of the Black Prince*
(Woodbridge, 1986).

Clifford J. Rogers, *The Wars of Edward III: Sources and
Interpretations* (Woodbridge, 1999) (also contains a selection
of important articles on the early stages of the Hundred
Years War).

A.R. Myers, ed., *English Historical Documents, iv, 1327–1485*
(London, 1969).

ADMINISTRATIVE AND GOVERNMENTAL RECORDS

Thomas Rymer, *Foedera, Conventiones, Litterae, etc.* (London,
1708–09); rev. ed. A. Clarke, F. Holbroke and J. Coley, 4
vols in 7 parts (Record Commission), 1816–69.

*Calendar of Close Rolls, Calendar of Patent Rolls, Calendar of
Inquisitions Post Mortem.*

For the household and estate of the Black Prince see M.C.B.
Dawes, ed., *The Black Prince's Register*, 4 vols (London,
1930–33).

Biographies of the Black Prince

Richard Barber, *Edward Prince of Wales and Aquitaine: A Biography of the Black Prince* (Woodbridge, 1978).

Barbara Emerson, *The Black Prince* (London, 1976).

M. Dupuy, *Le Prince Noir* (Paris, 1970).

David Green, *The Black Prince* (Stroud, 2001).

John Harvey, *The Black Prince and his Age* (London, 1976).

J. Moisant, *Le Prince Noir en Aquitaine, 1355–56, 1362–70* (Paris, 1894).

Military Studies

Andrew Ayton, *Knights and Warhorses: Military Service and the English Aristocracy under Edward III* (Woodbridge, 1994).

Andrew Ayton and J.L. Price, ed., *The Medieval Military Revolution: State and Society in Medieval and Early Modern Europe* (London and New York, 1995).

J. Barnie, *War in Medieval Society: Social Values and the Hundred Years War, 1337–99* (London, 1974).

Jim Bradbury, *The Medieval Siege* (Woodbridge, 1992).

A.H. Burne, *The Crécy War: A Military History of the Hundred Years War from 1337 to the Peace of Brétigny, 1360* (London, 1955).

Philippe Contamine, *Guerre, état et société à la fin du Moyen Age. Etudes sur les armées des rois de France, 1337–1494* (Paris, 1972); *War in the Middle Ages* (trans. Michael Jones) (Oxford, 1987).

Anne Curry and Michael Hughes, ed., *Arms, Armour and Fortifications in the Hundred Years War* (Woodbridge, 1994).

Kenneth Fowler, *Medieval Mercenaries* (London, 2000).

H.J. Hewitt, *The Black Prince's Expedition of 1355–1357* (Manchester, 1958); *The Organisation of War under Edward III, 1338–62* (Manchester, 1966).

Maurice Keen, ed., *Medieval Warfare: A History* (Oxford, 1999).

Michael Prestwich, *Armies and Warfare in the Middle Ages. The English Experience* (New Haven, 1996).

A.E. Prince, 'The Strength of English Armies in the Reign of

Edward III', *EHR*, xlvi (1931), 353–71.

Clifford J. Rogers, 'The Military Revolution of the Hundred Years' War', *Journal of Military History*, 57 (1993), 241–78; *War Cruel and Sharp: English Strategy under Edward III, 1327–1360* (Woodbridge, 2000).

J.M. Tourneur–Aumont, *La bataille de Poitiers (1356) et la construction de la France* (Paris, 1940).

T.F. Tout, 'Some Neglected Fights Between Crécy and Poitiers', *EHR*, xx (1905), 726–30.

Nicholas Wright, *Knights and Peasants. The Hundred Years War in the French Countryside* (Woodbridge, 1998).

STUDIES OF ARCHERY AND THE EFFICACY OF THE LONGBOW

M. Bennett, 'The Development of Battle Tactics in the Hundred Years War', *Arms, Armies and Fortifications*, ed. Curry and Hughes, 1–20.

Jim Bradbury, *The Medieval Archer* (New York, 1985).

Claude Gaier, 'L'invincibilité anglaise et le grande arc après la guerre de cent ans: un mythe tenace', *Tijdschrift voor gescheidenis*, 91 (1978), 378–85.

Robert Hardy, *The Longbow* (Cambridge, 1976).

John Keegan, *Face of Battle: A Study of Agincourt, Waterloo and the Somme* (Harmondsworth, 1978), 78–116.

Clifford J. Rogers, 'The Efficacy of the English Longbow: A Reply to Kelly DeVries', *War in History*, 5:2 (1998), 233–42.

GENERAL STUDIES

C. Allmand, *The Hundred Years War: England and France at War, c.1300–c.1450* (Cambridge, 1988).

F. Autrand, *Charles V, le sage* (Paris, 1994).

J. Bothwell, ed., *The Age of Edward III* (Woodbridge, 2001).

Pierre Capra, 'Les bases sociales du pouvoir anglo-gascon au milieu du xive siècle', *Le Moyen Age*, 4ème sér., 30 (1975), 273–99; 'L'évolution de l'administration anglo-gasconne au milieu du xive siècle', *Bordeaux et les Iles britanniques du xiiie au xxe siècle* [Actes du colloque franco-britannique tenu à York, 1973] (Bordeaux, 1975), 19–25.

Anne Curry, *The Hundred Years War* (Houndmills, 1993).

R. Delachenal, *Histoire de Charles V*, 5 vols (Paris, 1909–31).

Jean Favier, *La Guerre de Cent Ans* (Paris, 1980).

C. Given-Wilson, *The Royal Household and the King's Affinity: Service, Politics and Finance, 1360–1413* (New Haven and London, 1986); *The English Nobility in the Late Middle Ages* (London, 1987).

H.J. Hewitt, *Cheshire under the Three Edwards* (Chester, 1967).

M. Keen, *England in the Later Middle Ages* (London, 1973).

Margaret Wade Labarge, *Gascony. England's First Colony 1204–1453* (London, 1980).

W.M. Ormrod, *The Reign of Edward III. Crown and Political Society in England 1327–77* (New Haven and London, 1990).

M. Prestwich, *The Three Edwards: War and State in England 1272–1377* (London, 1980).

Jonathan Sumption, *The Hundred Years War, i: Trial by Battle* (London, 1990); *The Hundred Years War, ii: Trial by Fire* (London, 1999).

S.L. Waugh, *England in the Reign of Edward III* (Cambridge, 1991).

On Chivalry and Ransoms

D'A.J.D. Boulton, *The Knights of the Crown. The Monarchical Orders of Knighthood in Later Medieval Europe 1325–1520*, 2nd ed. (Woodbridge, 2000).

Hugh Collins, *The Order of the Garter, 1348–1461: Chivalry and Politics in Late Medieval England* (Oxford, 2000).

C. Given-Wilson and F. Beriac, 'Edward III's Prisoners of War: The Battle of Poitiers and its Context', *EHR*, cxvi (2001), 802–33.

M. Keen, *The Laws of War in the Late Middle Ages* (London, 1965); *Chivalry* (New Haven and London, 1984).

J. Vale, *Edward III and Chivalry: Chivalric Society and its Context,*

1270–1350 (Woodbridge, 1982).

M. Vale, *War and Chivalry: Aristocratic Culture in England, France and Burgundy at the End of the Middle Ages* (London, 1981); *The Princely Court: Medieval Courts and Culture in North-West Europe 1270–1380* (Oxford, 2001).

NOTES

INTRODUCTION – THE BLACK PRINCE AND THE HUNDRED YEARS WAR

1. The most recent biography of Edward of Woodstock is David Green, *The Black Prince* (Stroud, 2001).

1 – 1355, THE *GRANDE CHEVAUCHÉE*

1. *BPR*, iv, 143–5; H.J. Hewitt, *The Black Prince's Expedition of 1355–57* (Manchester, 1958), 21, 24. A.E. Prince, 'The Strength of English Armies in the Reign of Edward III', *EHR*, xlvi (1931), 353–71, estimated the men-at-arms brought by the chief captains to be as follows: Warwick, 120; Suffolk, 60; Salisbury, about 55; Cobham, 30; Lisle, 60. H.J. Hewitt, *The Organisation of War Under Edward III* (Manchester, 1966), 35, numbered Lisle's retinue as 20 knights, 39 esquires and 40 mounted archers, citing PRO E372/200/7. All manuscript references hereafter will be to the Public Record Office unless stated otherwise. In addition, Oxford may have had a contingent of 60 men-at-arms.

2. *BPR*, iii, 204–5, 214–16.

3. Hewitt, *Black Prince's Expedition*, 15, 17; R. Delachenal, *Histoire de Charles V* (5 vols) (Paris, 1909–31), i, 124 n. 4.

4. *BPR*, ii, 77; iv, 143–5; Clifford J. Rogers, *War Cruel and Sharp. English Strategy under Edward III, 1327–1360* (Woodbridge, 2000), 295 and n. 48; G.L. Harriss, *King, Parliament and Public Finance* (Oxford, 1975), 344–5. For the prince's appointment and duties as lieutenant see Rymer, III, i, 307, 312.

5. R. Barber, *Edward Prince of Wales and Aquitaine: A Biography of the Black Prince* (Woodbridge, 1978), 113–14, 276.

6. Hewitt, *Black Prince's Expedition*, 22–3, 80–1, 123; Delachenal, *Charles V*, i, 220–1.

7. *BPR*, iv, 157, 166–7.

8. Barber, *Edward*, 114.

9. C61/67/29; 8 Mar. 1355, *CCR, 1354–60*, 256; Rymer, III, i, 298–9, 302, 307–10, 323, 325. *BPR*, iv, 158, 160, 166; Thomas Carte, *Catalogue des rôles Gascons, Normans et Français dans les archives de la Tour de Londres*, 2 vols (London and Paris, 1746), i, 134.

10. C61/67/5; Kenneth Fowler, *The King's Lieutenant: Henry of Grosmont, First Duke of Lancaster* (London, 1969), 147; B. Emerson, *The Black Prince* (London, 1976), 90. For a tentative list of the ships arrested for the prince's use see

Hewitt, *Black Prince's Expedition*, 40–2. This excludes the cog *Saint Mary* of Winchelsea which, at 200 tons, was the largest ship in the fleet, E61/76/4; T.J. Runyan, 'Ships and Mariners in Later Medieval England', *Journal of British Studies*, 16:2 (1977), 2 n. 3. By 8 May, 44 ships were at Southampton for the prince's use, E101/26/37. Ships were arrested for Warwick's departure from 10 Mar. 1355, C61/67/14.

11. *BPR*, ii, 80–8; *ibid.*, iii, 212–6; *ibid.*, iv, 78, 158, 161; Hewitt, *Black Prince's Expedition*, 26.

12. Pierre Capra, 'Le séjour du Prince Noir, lieutenant du Roi, à l'Archévêché de Bordeaux (20 septembre 1355–11 avril 1357)', *Revue historique du Bordeaux et du département Gironde*, NS 7 (1958), 246–7; Margaret Wade Labarge, *Gascony. England's First Colony, 1204–1453* (London, 1980), 136–7; Hewitt, *Black Prince's Expedition*, 37. For the text of the oath and a list of witnesses see Henri Barckhausen, ed., *Livre de Coutumes* (Archives Municipales de Bordeaux), 1890, 439–44, 487.

13. The term was used in the context of the Black Death by Jean Favier, *La Guerre de Cent Ans* (Paris, 1980).

14. *CIPM*, x, no. 258; *GEC*, viii, 73–6; Jonathan Sumption, *The Hundred Years War, ii. Trial by Fire* (London, 1999), 175–6.

15. A.H. Burne, *The Crécy War: A Military History of the Hundred Years War from 1337 to the Peace of Brétigny, 1360* (London, 1955), 252; Henri Denifle, *La guerre de cent ans et la désolation des églises, monasteres et hospitaux en France* (Paris, 1902), ii, 86. See also Pierre Tucoo-Chala, *Gaston Fébus et la vicomté de Béarn (1343–1391)* (Bordeaux, 1959), 70. If not before, the prince and Gaston met on 17 Nov., Geoffrey Le Baker, *Chronicon Galfridi le Baker de Swynebroke, 1303–56*, ed. E.M. Thompson (Oxford, 1889), 128, 135, 138; Hewitt, *Black Prince's Expedition*, 45; Delachenal, *Charles V*, i, 128 n.1.

16. Barber, *Edward*, 119; Sumption, *Hundred Years War, ii*, 181–4; Emerson, *Black Prince*, 94, 97–8; Hewitt, *Black Prince's Expedition*, 69, 76; J.M. Touneur-Aumont, *La bataille de Poitiers (1356) et la construction de la France* (Paris,

1940), 65. Delachenal, *Charles V*, i, 127–8.

17. Clifford J. Rogers, 'Edward III and the Dialectics of Strategy', *TRHS*, 6th ser., 4 (1994), 100–1.

18. Robert of Avesbury, *De gestis mirabilis regis Edwardi tertii*, ed. E.M. Thompson, 1889, 445–7; R. Barber, ed., *Life and Campaigns of the Black Prince* (Woodbridge, 1986), 53.

19. Françoise Lehoux, *Jean de France, duc de Berri. Sa vie. Son action politique (1340–1416)* (Paris, 1966), i, 57; Pierre-Clément Timbal, *La Guerre de Cent Ans vue à travers les registres du Parlement, 1337–1369* (Paris, 1961), 108–9.

2 – Winter/Spring 1355–56 – Defence and Preparation

1. Sumption, *Hundred Years War*, ii, 190.

2. See K. Fowler, 'Letters and Dispatches of the Fourteenth Century', *Guerre et société en France, en Angleterre et en Bourgogne XIVe–XVe siècle*s, ed. Philippe Contamine, Charles Giry-Deloison and Maurice Keen (Lille, 1991), 77–8, 80, nn. 69–76; A.K. McHardy, 'Some Reflections on Edward III's Use of Propaganda', *The Age of Edward III*, ed. J. Bothwell (Woodbridge, 2001), 171–92.

3. C61/68/4; C66/68/4; 24 Oct. 1356, *BPR*, iv, 192; John of Reading, *Chronica Johannis de Reading et Anonymi Cantuarensis 1346–1367*, ed. James Tait (Manchester, 1914), 120; Avesbury, 437, 439.

4. *Register of John de Trillek, Bishop of Hereford (A.D. 1344–1361)* ed. Joseph H. Parry (Hereford, 1910–12), 242; Jean Froissart, *Oeuvres*, ed. K. de Lettenhove (Brussels, 1867–77), xviii, 389–92; *Chronicle of London from 1089 to 1483*, ed. E. Tyrrell and N.H. Nicolas (London, 1827), 204–8; Delachenal, *Charles V*, ii, 381–4; *Life and Campaigns*, ed. Barber, 57–9.

5. Froissart, *Oeuvres*, ed. Lettenhove, v, 528–9; *Chartulary of Winchester Cathedral*, ed. A.W. Goodman (Winchester, 1927), 159–61, no. 370, 162–4, no. 371; Fowler, 'Letters and Dispatches', 77–8; Delachenal, *Charles V*, i, 205–6; Hewitt, *Black Prince's Expedition*, 79.

6. 7 Feb. 1356, Rymer, III, i, 322; Henxteworth ff. 13, 21, 25.

7. 15, 26 Mar. 1356, *BPR*, iii, 224, 225; Rymer, III, i, 315; Hewitt, *Black Prince's Expedition*, 21.

8. C61/70/4; 71/7; Burne, *Crécy War*, 276; Barber, *Edward*, 129–30; Emerson, *Black Prince*, 102; Capra, 'Le séjour du Prince Noir', 245.

9. Nicholas Wright, *Knights and Peasants. The Hundred Years War in the French Countryside* (Woodbridge, 1998), 34–5.

10. Sumption, *Hundred Years War, ii*, 193.

3 – THE CAMPAIGN OF 1356

1. E36/278/88; *BPR*, iv, 145; Rymer, III, i, 325, 333; Fowler, *King's Lieutenant*, 153–5.

2. Barber, *Edward*, 131–2; Hewitt, *Black Prince's Expedition*, 102.

3. Delachenal, *Charles V*, i, 192–7; Robert Hardy, 'The Longbow', *Arms, Armies and Fortifications in the Hundred Years War*, ed. A. Curry and M. Hughes (Woodbridge, 1994), 163; P.J. Morgan, *War and Society in Medieval Cheshire, 1277–1403* (Manchester, 1987), 111, 113.

4. On French military recruitment and organisation see Philippe Contamine, *Guerre, état et société à la fin du moyen âge. Études sur les armées des rois de France, 1337–1494* (Paris, 1972), 26–64.

5. Denifle, *La désolation*, ii, 112–21; Fowler, *King's Lieutenant*, 154; Emerson, *Black Prince*, 108–9.

6. Letter to the mayor, aldermen and commons of London, 22 October, *Life and Campaigns*, ed. Barber, 57.

7. Jean Froissart, *Chroniques*, ed. S. Luce (SHF) (Paris, 1870–), v, 414–16; Delachenal, *Charles V*, i, 190, 225–6; Barber, *Edward*, 134, 136–7; Burne, *Crécy War*, 276–8; Hewitt, *Black Prince's Expedition*, 104, 107–9; Labarge, *Gascony*, 139–41.

4 – THE BATTLE OF POITIERS

1. *Chronique de règnes de Jean II et de Charles V*, ed. R. Delachenal (SHF) (Paris, 1910), 72.

2. *Life and Campaigns*, ed. Barber, 58.

3. Le Baker, *Chronicon*, 147; Rogers, *War Cruel and Sharp*, 379 and n. 160.

4. Hewitt, *Black Prince's Expedition*, 121; Delachenal, *Charles V*, i, 222 and n. 3. It may well be the case that only about half of Orléans' soldiers departed with him although a number of the survivors of earlier attacks joined him, Rogers, *War Cruel and Sharp*, 380.

5. Not only was the fall of the standard indicative of a collapse on the battlefield it was also used frequently in iconography to emphasise the outcome of an encounter, such as in the Breslau Froissart manuscript, Laurence Harf-Lancner, 'The Illustration of Book 1 of Froissart's *Chroniques*', *Froissart Across the Genres*, ed. Donald Maddox and Sara-Sturm-Maddox (Gainesville, 1998), 238.

6. *Froissart's Chronicles*, ed. and trans. J. Jolliffe (London, 1967), 175; Froissart, *Oeuvres*, ed. Lettenhove, v, 461, 463.

7. The maps are based on 3615 IGN (No. 1727 E. Poitiers −4− Série Bleue). The positioning of the hedge and ditch and the extent of the wood and marsh/es are conjectural.

8. Clifford J. Rogers, ed., *The Wars of Edward III: Sources and Interpretations* (Woodbridge, 1999), 163–4; Froissart, *Oeuvres*, ed. Lettenhove, xviii, 385–7; *Life and Campaigns*, ed. Barber, 57–9.

9. *Wars of Edward III*, ed. Rogers, 165–6.

10. *Life and Campaigns*, ed. Barber, 75–6.

11. *Froissart: Chronicles*, ed. and trans. Brereton, 128; Froissart, *Chroniques*, ed. Luce, v, 21–2.

12. Contamine, *Guerre, état et société*, 45, 175. It was not the only such attack on the French aristocracy, see B.L. Cotton Caligula D III f. 33; Froissart, *Oeuvres*, ed. Lettenhove, xviii, 388.

13. Delachenal, *Charles V*, i, 220. N.B. according to Le Baker, *Chronicon*, 151, French crossbows at Poitiers did considerable damage.

14. M. Bennett, 'The Development of Battle Tactics in the Hundred Years War', *Arms, Armies and Fortifications*, ed. Curry and Hughes, 7–9 and n. 18.

5 – Aftermath: Prisoners and the treaties of London and Brétigny

1. For what follows see C. Given-Wilson and F. Beriac, 'Edward III's Prisoners of War: The Battle of Poitiers and its Context', *EHR*, cxvi (2001), 802–33; Given-Wilson, *Royal Household*, 87.

2. D'A.J.D. Boulton, *The Knights of the Crown. The Monarchical Orders of Knighthood in Later Medieval Europe 1325–1520*, 2nd ed. (Woodbridge, 2000), 96–166 (on the Garter) 167–210 (on the Star) esp. 191–3. See also Hugh Collins, *The Order of the Garter, 1348–1461: Chivalry and Politics in Late Medieval England* (Oxford, 2000). For Mauron see Le Baker, *Chronicon*, 120, the English forces were commanded by Walter Bentley and Robert Knolles who states only 45 were numbered among the captured and the slain.

3. *Anonimalle Chronicle*, 40–1; Froissart, *Chroniques*, ed. Luce, v, 82–3.

4. Wright, *Knights and Peasants*, 51.

5. Rymer, III, ii, 1; A.R. Myers, ed., *English Historical Documents, iv, 1327–1485* (London, 1969), 103–8.

Conclusion – Poitiers, the Black Prince and his Military Retinue

1. Froissart, *Chroniques*, ed. Luce, v, 42.

2. Nigel Saul, *Death, Art and Memory in Medieval England. The Cobham Family and their Monuments, 1300–1500* (Oxford, 2001), 160.

3. Saul, *Death, Art and Memory*, 149–68.

4. Froissart, *Chroniques*, ed. Luce, v, 60.

5. Matteo Villani, *Historia Universalis,* ed. L.A. Muratori (1729), 419.

6. Favier, *La Guerre de Cent Ans*, 212.

7. Anne Curry, 'Richard II and the War with France', *The Reign of Richard II*, ed. Gwilym Dodd (Stroud, 2000), 35. For the conception of the Hundred Years War as a war of

three treaties see Anne Curry, *The Hundred Years War* (Houndmills, 1993), 152–5.

<h2 style="text-align:center">APPENDIX 2 – DRAMATIS PERSONAE</h2>

1. For biographical collections see George F. Beltz, *Memorials of the Most Noble Order of the Garter* (London, 1841); G. Dupont-Ferrier, *Gallia Regia ou état des officiers royaux des bailliages et des sénéchaussées de 1328 à 1515* (Paris, 1942); R.H. Fritze and William B. Robison, ed., *Historical Dictionary of Late Medieval England, 1272–1485* (Connecticut and London, 2002); R.A. Griffiths, ed., *The Principality of Wales in the Later Middle Ages: The Structure and Personnel of Government, i: South Wales, 1277–1536* (Cardiff, 1972); N.H. Nicolas, *The Controversy between Sir Richard Scrope and Sir Robert Grosvenor in the Court of Chivalry*, 2 vols (London, 1832); P.H.W. Booth and A. Carr, ed., *The Account of Master John de Brunham the Younger, Chamberlain of Chester of the Revenues of the Counties of Chester and Flint 1361–62* (Record Society of Lancashire and Cheshire), 1991; J. Roskell, L. Clarke and C. Rawcliffe, ed., *History of Parliament, 1386–1421*, 4 vols (Stroud, 1993); *Dictionnaire de biographie française* (Paris, 1933); *Dictionary of National Biography*, 63 vols (London, 1885–1900). For further details on the members of the Black Prince's household and retinue where full references are given see David S. Green, 'The Household and Military Retinue of Edward the Black Prince', Unpub. PhD thesis, University of Nottingham, 1998; 'The Military Personnel of Edward the Black Prince', *Medieval Prosopography*, 21 (2000), 133–52; 'The Later Retinue of Edward the Black Prince', *Nottingham Medieval Studies*, xliv (2000), 141–51; 'Politics and Service with Edward the Black Prince', *Age of Edward III*, ed. Bothwell, 53–68.

2. Gabriel Loirette, 'Arnaud-Amanieu, sire d'Albret et ses rapports avec la monarchie française pendant le règne de Charles V (1336–80)', *Annales du Midi*, xlii (1931), 5–39; Chandos Herald, *Life of the Black Prince*, ed. Pope and

Lodge, 237.

3. *Knighton's Chronicle, 1337–96*, ed. G. Martin (Oxford, 1995), 22; see also Adam Murimuth, *Continuatio Chronicarum*, ed. E.M. Thompson (London, 1889), 121; Sumption, *Hundred Years' War*, ii, 330–8; M. Dupuy, *Le Prince Noir* (Paris, 1970), 298.

4. Chandos Herald, *Life of the Black Prince*, ed. Pope and Lodge, 237; M. Keen, *The Laws of War in the Late Middle Ages* (London, 1965), 84. This included service at the siege of Limoges, *Froissart: Chronicles*, ed. G. Brereton (Harmondsworth, repr. 1978), 176, 219, 227.

5. Dupont-Ferrier, *Gallia Regia*, iv, 527; Beltz, *Memorials*, 182–7; Chandos Herald, *Life of the Black Prince*, ed. Pope and Lodge, 237–8.

6. *DBF*, iii, 655–8; Dupont-Ferrier, *Gallia Regia*, v, 233.

7. Dupuy, *Prince Noir*, 307; Chandos Herald, *Life of the Black Prince*, 238.

8. Thanks to Michael Jones for providing his notes on James Audley for the forthcoming *DNB*. See also Griffiths, *Principality*, 114, 210, 553; Chandos Herald, *Life of the Black Prince*, ed. Pope and Lodge, 238; Dupont-Ferrier, *Gallia Regia*, iv, 474.

9. *DBF*, iv, 458–9.

10. Beltz, *Memorials*, 159–62; *GEC*, ii, 3–6.

11. *Knighton's Chronicle*, ed. Martin, 60–4, 142, 144; *BPR*, iv, 338; Barber, *Edward*, 114; W.M. Ormrod, *The Reign of Edward III. Crown and Political Society in England, 1327–1377* (New Haven and London, 1990), 103.

12. *Knighton's Chronicle*, ed. Martin, 172; Barber, *Edward*, 143, 153, 162.

13. *DBF*, viii, 298–9.

14. Barber *Edward*, 162; *DNB*, iv, 43–4.

15. *DNB*, x, 43–4; Given-Wilson, *Household and Affinity*, 72; Le Baker, *Chronicon*, 136, 140, 298; Froissart, *Chroniques*, vi, ed. Luce, lxviii, 150; *Chroniques des quatre premiers Valois (1327–1393)*, ed. S. Luce (SHF) (Paris, 1862), 159, 172; Dupont-Ferrier, *Gallia Regia*, iv, 474. For the battle at Lussac bridge see *Chronique Normande du XIVe siècle*, ed. E. et A. Molinier (SHF) (Paris, 1882), 194.

16. Chandos said 'Dan Bertran, quant je vous prins en Bretaigne, vous jurastes que vous ne vous armeriez point contr le prince, si le roy de France ou ses freres n'avoient guerre contre le prince ou contre le roy d'Angleterre.' Lors respondi monseigneur Bertran à monseigneur Jehan de Chandos, present le prince disant: 'A Dieu le vou, ja dittes vous veoir! Mais monseigneur le prince n'a cy point de guerre; ains s'est armé du parti du roy Petre...', *Chronique des quatre premiers Valois*, 181.

17. R. Kaeuper and E. Kennedy, *The* Book of Chivalry *of Geoffroi de Charny: Text, Context and Translation* (Philadelphia, 1996).

18. Booth and Carr, *Account of Master John de Brunham*, 128.

19. *DBF*, viii, 1490–1.

20. It is possible that he was the son and heir of another Reginald as suggested by John Wickham Fraser, 'Notices of the Family of Cobham of Sterborough Castle, Lingfield, Surrey', *Surrey Archaeological Collections*, ii (1894), 119; Chandos Herald, *Life of the Black Prince*, ed. Pope and Lodge, 243; Barber, *Edward*, 114, 170; Saul, *Death, Art and Memory*, 124–36.

21. E101/28/8; L. Mirot et E. Déprez, 'Les ambassades anglaises pendant la guerre de cent ans', *Bibliothèque des écoles des chartes*, lxx (1899), 27, 28, 32; Rymer, III, i, 504.

22. For further details see *VCH*, Oxon, vi, 60, 69, 334–6; Griffiths, *Principality*, 229–30.

23. *BPR*, iv, 133; Denholm-Young, *Country Gentry*, 128.

24. Beltz, *Memorials*, 140–2; *CIPM*, xiv, 214–27, no. 209; Lincoln Archives Office Reg. xii, fo. 163.

25. *DNB*, vi, 1173–4; Beltz, *Memorials*, 274–9; Dupuy, *Prince Noir*, 307; *GEC*, v, 292–3 and n. E.

26. The *DNB* account conflates William II and William III. See also Dupont-Ferrier, *Gallia Regia*, iv, 474; S. Luce, *Histoire de Bertrand Du Guesclin et son époque: La jeunesse de Bertrand (1320–1364)* (Paris, 1896), 405–6; Delachenal, *Charles V*, ii, 355 n. 3; Froissart, *Oeuvres*, ed. Lettenhove, xxi, 187.

27. Chandos Herald, *Life of the Black Prince*, ed. Pope and Lodge, 84–7, 158–9.

28. *Chronicle of Jean de Venette*, ed. and trans. J. Birdsall and R.A. Newhall (New York, 1953), 138.

29. *The Chronicle of Adam Usk, 1377–1421*, ed. C. Given-Wilson (Oxford, 1997), 73 and n. 6, also see 'Annales Ricardi Secundi et Henrici Quarti', *Johannis de Trokelowe et Anon Chronica et Annales*, ed. H.T. Riley (Rolls Ser.) (London, 1866), 287–8; *Gallia Regia*, iii, 541; iv, 474; v, 289 no. 20079; Chandos Herald, *Life of the Black Prince*, ed., Pope and Lodge, 246.

30. Chandos Herald, *Life of the Black Prince*, ed., Pope and Lodge, 247; Dupont-Ferrier, *Gallia Regia*, iii, 510–11.

31. Beltz, *Memorials*, 28–33; Chandos Herald, *Life of the Black Prince*, ed., Pope and Lodge, 241; Jean le Bel, *Chronique*, ed. J. Viard and E. Déprez (Paris, 1904–05), ii, 260–2; 137–8; *Chronicle of Jean de Venette*, 262–3.

32. *Chronicle of Jean de Venette*, 121–2, 134, 295; Delachenal, *Charles V*, iii, 38–60.

33. Griffiths, *Principality*, 119, 122; *VCH*, Berks; 298, 331; iv, 239; *BPR*, iii; 198–9, 383; iv, 285, 364; *CCR, 1369–74*; 68; Roskell *et al.*, *History of Parliament*, iii, 517–19.

34. Beltz, *Memorials*, 65–8.

35. Froissart, *Oeuvres*, ed. Lettenhove, iii, 197.

36. It is uncertain if he fought in the prince's division at Crécy as suggested by J. Vale, *Edward III and Chivalry: Chivalric Society and its Context, 1270–1350* (Woodbridge, 1982), 153.

37. In 1364 he received Garter robes, of which there is a picture in a St Alban's manuscript, S.M. Newton, *Fashion in the Age of the Black Prince. A Study of the Years 1340–1365* (Woodbridge, 1988), 45.

38. On 24 Oct. 1362 (see 7 May 1360) Edward III appointed Richard Stafford, John Chandos, Stephen Cosington, Nigel Loryng, Richard Totesham, Adam Hoghton and William Felton 'to crave, receive and retain' those lands, as required by the treaty of Brétigny, *CCR, 1360–4*, 359. There is a further reference to his appointment as the king's deputy in France dated 1 July 1362, *ibid., 1364–8*, 128.

39. Froissart, *Oeuvres*, ed. Lettenhove, vi, 394.

40. *DNB*, xiii, 661–2; Booth and Carr, *Account of Master John*

de Brunham, 169–70; *GEC*, xi, 388–90.

41. Griffiths, *Principality*, 105; T.F. Tout, *Chapters in the Administrative History of Mediaeval England. The Wardrobe, the Chamber and the Small Seal* (Manchester, 1920–33), iii, 296, 327–8; *ibid.*, v, 390 n. 2, 439–40; Booth and Carr, *Account of Master John de Brunham*, 175; *DNB*, liii, 456–8; v, 390.

42. *Scrope-Grosvenor*, 240–3.

43. 10 Mar. 1353, *BPR*, ii, 45–6.

44. *GEC*, xii, pt. 1, 429–32; pt. 2, 151.

45. *GEC*, x, 222–4.

46. This was argued against by Bernard de la Troy, whose statement was witnessed by Clisson, Montague, Burghersh, Robert Holland, Thomas Roos and Brocas, BL Cotton Caligula D III f.102.

47. P.H.W. Booth states that he joined the prince shortly after the Black Death, *The Financial Administration of the Lordship and County of Cheshire, 1272–1377* (Chetham Society, 3rd ser., xxviii, 1981), 74. Tout notes him as steward from *c.*1350 and governor of the prince's business from at least 29 Sept. 1358 until his death in 1361, *Chapters*, v, 387, 391, 433, 440.

INDEX

43, 44, 46, 63, 73, 101,
107, 111, 113, 114, 116,
119, 120, 122

Guesclin, Bertrand du, 18, 19,
69, 99, 100, 101, 107, 115,
116, 121

Henry V, 14, 17, 80, 83

Henxteworth, John, 27, 90

Jacquerie, 18, 61, 74, 77, 117

Jean II 'the Good' (1350–64),
16, 45, 46, 49, 53, 54, 55,
71, 72, 73, 76, 82, 83, 88,
91, 92, 94, 104, 108, 111

Kentwode, John, 118–19

Knolles, Robert, 18, 43, 97,
116

Lisle, John (d. 1355), 23, 27,
32, 86

Loryng, Nigel, 27, 38, 58, 89,
112, 113, 119–20, 122

Montague, William, earl of
Salisbury, 23, 24, 27, 37,
40, 52, 53, 59, 60, 62, 86,
89, 110, 119, 121–2, 126

Montfort, Jean de, 18, 43,
101, 107

Pedro I 'the Cruel', king of
Castile, 19, 20, 99, 100,
101, 107, 116

Pole, de la, Michael, 128

Reims (expedition and
campaign, 1359–60), 15,
16, 68, 74–5, 99, 101, 103,
104, 107, 109, 111, 116,
117, 120, 124, 125, 127

Rivers
Ariège, 33, 34
Charente, 40
Cher, 46, 47

Dordogne, 33, 40, 110
Garonne, 33, 41
Gers, 33
Indre, 47
Loire, 46, 47, 110
Lot, 21
Miosson, 48, 50, 53, 58

Stafford, Richard, 25, 27, 28,
32, 38, 39, 44, 86, 90, 122

Star, Company of the, 72, 108

Sully, John, 123

Treaties
Anglo-Castilian (1363), 111
Bordeaux (1357), 73, 112
Brétigny-Calais (1360), 16,
17, 64, 75, 76, 83, 99, 105,
107, 111, 113, 114, 116,
120, 121, 128
Guînes (1354), 22
1st Treaty of London (1358),
73, 74, 76
2nd Treaty of London
(1359), 73, 74
Paris (1259), 13, 83
Troyes (1420), 83

Trussel, William, 27, 89, 110,
124

Ufford, Robert, earl of Suffolk,
23, 24, 27, 30, 37, 40, 48,
52, 53, 62, 86, 89, 124

Ufford, Thomas, 114

Vere, John, earl of Oxford, 23,
24, 40, 52, 53, 62, 86, 89,
124–5

Wales, 17, 24, 39, 86, 113,
119, 122

Warre, Roger de la, 125–6

Wingfield, John, 28, 38, 90

THE BATTLE FOR YORK: MARSTON MOOR 1644
JOHN BARRATT

A major new history of the largest battle of the English Civil Wars, where 40,000
troops fought on Marston Moor, six miles west of the city of York.

208pp 115 illus (28 col.) Paperback
£16.99/$24.99   ISBN 0 7524 2335 5

THE BATTLE FOR ABERDEEN 1644

CHRIS BROWN

The first-ever history of the battle for Aberdeen fought during the British Civil Wars.

128pp 72 illus. Paperback
£12.99/$18.99   ISBN 0 7524 2340 1

FLODDEN 1513

Niall Barr

'enthralling... reads as thrillingly as a novel.' *THE SCOTS MAGAZINE*
'an engrossing account of the battle... exemplary.' *BBC HISTORY MAGAZINE*

176pp 74 illus. (23 col.) Paperback
£14.99/$24.99   ISBN 0 7524 1792 4

BOSWORTH 1485: PSYCHOLOGY OF A BATTLE
MICHAEL K. JONES

'Transforms our understanding of what actually happened on that fateful day'
PROFESSOR A.J. POLLARD

272pp 100 illus. (30 col.) Hardback
£25/$29.99   ISBN 0 7524 2334 7

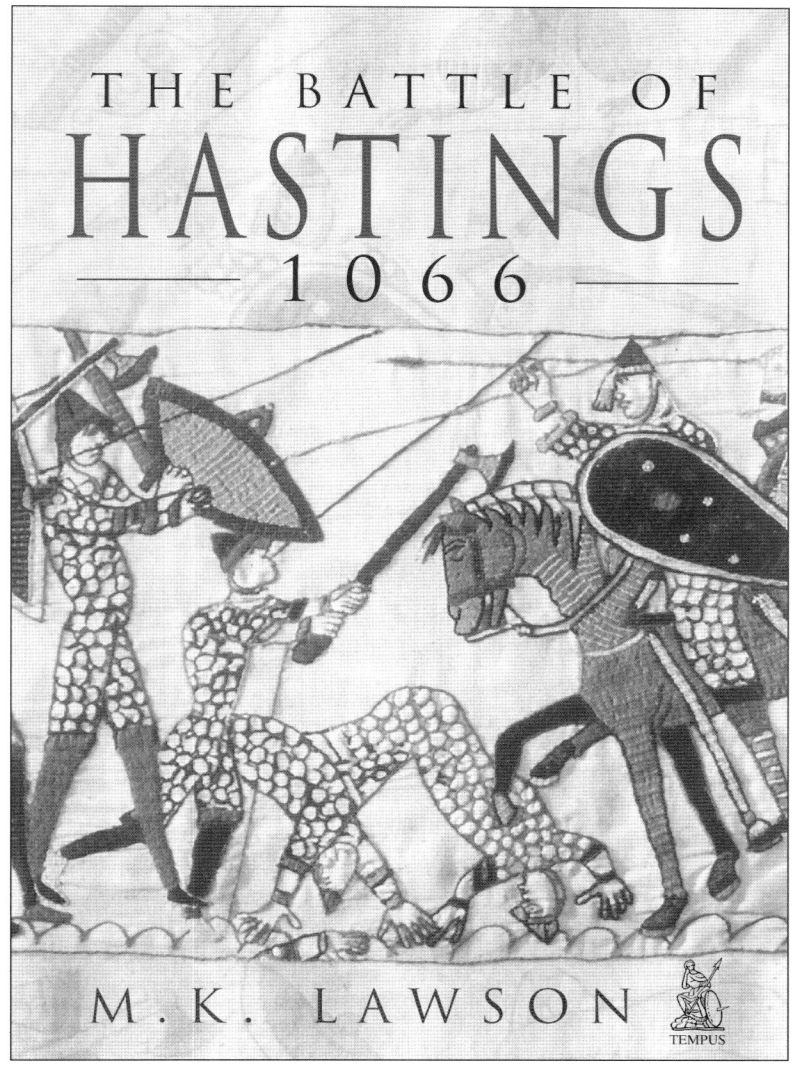

THE BATTLE OF HASTINGS 1066

M.K. LAWSON

A new history of the most decisive battle in English history.

304pp 120 illus. (21 col.) Paperback

£16.99/$24.99   ISBN 0 7524 1998 6